JOACHIM SPLICHAL'S
Patina Cookbook

Spuds, Truffles and Wild Gnocchi

WITH TEXT BY CHARLES PERRY

CollinsPublishersSanFrancisco

A Division of HarperCollinsPublishers

First published in 1995 by Collins Publishers San Francisco
1160 Battery Street, San Francisco, CA 94111

Recipes by Joachim Splichal
Text by Charles Perry
Black-and-White Photography by David Stork
Color Photography by Patrice Meigneux
Recipe Testing by Brigit Legere Binns
Design by James Cross
Edited by Meesha Halm

Library of Congress Cataloging-in-Publication Data

Splichal, Joachim.
    Joachim Splichal's Patina cookbook: spuds, truffles and wild
gnocchi / with text by Charles Perry.
        p. cm.— (Great chefs — great restaurants)

    Includes index.

    ISBN 0-00-255474-7
    1. Cookery, American. 2. Splichal, Joachim. 3. Patina (Restaurant)
I. Perry, Charles II. Title. III. Title: Patina cookbook. IV . Series

    TX715.S7567   1995
    641.5973 – dc20   94-40851
                    CIP

Printed in China
10 9 8 7 6 5 4 3 2 1

Contents

INTRODUCTION
7

MARKETS / COLD APPETIZERS
9

MORNING / HOT APPETIZERS
24

LUNCH / SOUPS
58

EARLY SATURDAY NIGHT, KITCHEN / FISH MAIN COURSES
66

EARLY SATURDAY NIGHT, FRONT OF THE HOUSE / MEAT MAIN COURSES
86

LATER SATURDAY NIGHT, KITCHEN / POULTRY AND GAME BIRD MAIN COURSES
109

PASTRY KITCHEN / DESSERTS
121

CLOCK OUT
135

BASIC RECIPES AND TECHNIQUES
136

METRIC CONVERSIONS AND RESOURCES
140

ACKNOWLEDGMENTS
141

INDEX
142

To my wife Christine,

without whom none of this would be possible.

Introduction

In 1981 Joachim Splichal came to Los Angeles to work in a private club. Within two years, as this young German chef moved on to a downtown restaurant called the 7th Street Bistro, and then to his Max au Triangle in Beverly Hills, he became one of the most talked-about new chefs in town, widely acknowledged as one of the most daring innovators of that swashbuckling age. His "ravioli," for example, was a dessert – phyllo stuffed with raspberries and served in almond and apricot sauce – while his "napoleon" was an appetizer layered with vegetables. And could this be a terrine – pasta layered with corn and lobster?

Joachim Splichal seemed to give off sparks. People came to his restaurants to be astonished, and many other young chefs, taking note, tried to imitate his radical ingenuity. The result: the extremes of wackiness that Los Angeles restaurants soon became known for. Splichal's own background is entirely classical. Setting out from his hometown, Spaichingen, in the southern part of Germany, he made the traditional pilgrimage that every European-trained chef is obliged to make, from one exacting French restaurant kitchen to another. Before coming to California, he was sous-chef at Jacques Maximin's Chantecler in Nice. So his startling innovations were solidly based on sound technique and intellectual integrity.

The firm foundation became more evident when he opened Patina in Hollywood in 1989. The menus, written in his wry, whimsical manner (for example, "soup of yesterday" instead of "soupe du jour"), now had a homely quality. He showed special affection for the humbler vegetables, such as the lowly turnip, and he championed unfashionable cuts of meat. One section of the menu was entitled "Odd Things," and some of those things – such as cockscombs – seemed very odd indeed, though in fact, cockscombs are very much a part of the classical French cuisine.

His exploration of the potato was emblematic of his interest in neglected foods. In the 1980s many chefs were rediscovering the potato, but they were making it into purees or ostentatiously lumpy homestyle mashed potatoes. Splichal treated the spud like a kind of pasta, or made it the base for a sauce. Some of his dishes featured potatoes in two, or even three, configurations. The former wild man became known as L.A.'s Potatomeister, Idaho's best-loved Californian.

People come to Patina, and to the Pinot Bistro, its sister restaurant in the San Fernando Valley, for the same reasons that drew them to Splichal's earlier restaurants – to marvel at his skill and to enjoy the buzz of a happening place where celebrities are regulars. There's also the fact that Patina seems to be becoming more European, with a greater emphasis on cultivating lifelong patrons. All restaurants have VIPs, but at Patina, there's a category called JBSes (from Splichal's initials) – loyal customers who get especially careful treatment.

Diners in their comfortable chairs have little idea what it takes for their food to reach them. In the case of a restaurant with Patina's standards, it takes not only ability and coordination but also the creative tension supplied by Joachim Splichal, a restless guy who nevertheless has "consistency, consistency, consistency" as his motto.

5:30 a.m. *Gray dawn.*

In most of the city it's much too early for the snooze alarm, but the Los Angeles Produce Market has been bustling since just after midnight. Even now an occasional truck threads its way through the floodlit warehouse islands and noses up to a loading dock, like an airliner taxiing up to a terminal. Twice a week a *Patina* employee shops for produce here in the wee hours. Today, however, **Joachim Splichal** and his executive chef, Jonny Fernow, want to see for themselves what's available this season. Dodging the traffic – pallets of produce being trundled off trucks, special orders being wheeled among wholesalers on hand trucks – they walk through cluttered displays of *Chinese* mushrooms and white eggplants that are exactly the size of eggs. *Kauai* mangos (you bet they are; each one is wrapped in a page from the island's newspaper). Yellow limes, brilliant red peppers, brussels sprouts covered with chunks of ice to keep them fresh. The sudden pungency of onions. The staggering scent of fresh herbs.

Joachim finds *fraises de bois* – tiny, fragrant, homely looking European strawberries. "How much?" he asks the dealer. "I could make sorbet with them. Give me two cases for Friday." He and the dealer discuss the grower. "There's a Swiss guy," Joachim says. "He supplies all the Riviera with fraises de bois. This guy should get in contact with him, the climate here is the same as the Riviera."

$7{:}00$ a.m. The floor at Fish Warehouse Seafood is being washed and squeegeed. Boxes of seafood on ice are all around: flounder, *striped bass*, New Zealand snapper, shiny John Dorys with spotted sides. Beautiful salmon, striking red rock cod, hideously ugly *monkfish*. In the refrigerated cutting room men in white overalls and hairnets are filleting fish to work orders pinned on the wall. One man is laboriously removing pinbones from a *salmon* fillet with needlenose pliers.

Joachim chats in French with the boss, a young guy wearing a University of Cannes T-shirt. "So when do you open your cafe downtown?" the guy asks. "I don't know," Joachim says. "It keeps going back and forth. By November 15th, maybe."

They walk into a very cold refrigerated room where larger fish are kept. The yellowish fins on the backs and bellies of the plump big-eye tuna look like giant cartoony sawteeth. The carcasses of *New Zealand swordfish* are like big gray tree trunks. The boss remarks, "It's quiet today. You come on a Friday, you'll see how busy it gets. **Fridays, we're walking on fish**."

8:00 a.m.

Like a lot of L.A.'s meat industry, K&M Meat Packing Co. is located in Vernon, an industrial community near downtown. K&M's neighbors are fabric cutters, cardboard carton fabricators, import-export warehouses. This is a neighborhood of railway spurs and dead-end streets ending in big turnarounds for trailer trucks.

Joachim and the boss are standing on the loading dock. "There's a glut of farmed salmon," says the boss, "so the wild salmon aren't moving very well." The dock is full of cardboard cartons of meat, but meat can't be treated as casually as cardboard might imply (a posted yellow sign declares the Vernon City Code: "Food For Resale Shall Be Transported In Health Department Approved Vehicles Only"). When Joachim and the boss go into the cutting rooms, they put on white overcoats and hairnets that look like sloppy chefs' toques made of the world's cheesiest cheesecloth.

Leading from the dock are overhead racks designed for slinging a side of beef onto, but these days whole carcasses are rare. Now the meat is usually broken down first at the slaughterhouses into "primal cuts." In the chilly cutting room, which has an indescribable damp aroma, the primal cuts are broken down still further.

One table is for red meat, the other for *chicken*. When a butcher finishes a chicken, he casually **lobs** the pieces where they should go in perfect arcs. A specialist scrupulously trims all the fat off the *filets mignons* he's slicing. The vacuum-sealed plastic packages go into cardboard cartons, and a worker with a felt-tip pen checks off one of the squares on the box to indicate the contents: say, beef sirloin peeled 7-up, or restredy rib 18-109.

Joachim and the boss talk meat; they talk tongue, and the difficulty of getting restaurant diners to go for it, what a shame. *Smoked tongue*, maybe they'll eat; people don't seem to think of it as tongue.

The boss also wants to know when Joachim's new place, Cafe Pinot will open. This plunges Joachim into the complicated business of opening a new restaurant – dealing with the permits, the menu concept, all the last-minute delays. To say nothing of all the other projects in the hopper – still another new restaurant being planned, the menu he's creating for a cruise-ship line. Joachim sighs. **"I'm thinking now..." He pauses, then says at last, "I'm thinking now maybe in January."**

66

I've been very influenced by the ethnic things I found in California. For instance, 12 years ago I wouldn't touch sushi, but I ended
up making sushi with potato. Because of the ethnic richness here, chefs play around more here than they do in Europe. I think the playing
around is fun, but I also think the dish has to make sense.

99

Ahi Tuna Tower

WITH AVOCADO, PLUM TOMATO AND YELLOW BELL PEPPER

SERVES 4

I use a 2-inch-diameter plastic pipe specially cut in 5-inch lengths to create these colorful towers of ahi tuna and vegetables. By removing the top and bottom of eight of the smallest cans available (such as those that contain jalapeño peppers or tomato paste), you can achieve almost the same stunning result.

Plum Tomato Mousse

1 1/2 cups peeled and seeded ripe plum tomatoes (about 7 tomatoes)
2 tablespoons extra virgin olive oil
Salt and freshly ground white pepper

In a food processor fitted with the metal blade or in a blender, process the tomatoes until very smooth. Place the puréed tomatoes in a strainer lined with slightly dampened cheesecloth over a bowl. Cover the strainer loosely with plastic wrap and allow to drain overnight in the refrigerator. In a small mixing bowl, stir together tomato mousse with the olive oil, salt and pepper to taste, and blend well. Set aside, covered, until ready to assemble the dish.

Ahi Towers

6 ounces top-quality ahi tuna, cut into 1/4-inch dice
1 tablespoon finely chopped chives
1 medium shallot, finely chopped
1 cup peeled and seeded plum tomatoes (see page 139), cut into 1/2-inch cubes
    (about 4 tomatoes)
Salt and freshly ground white pepper
1/2 large avocado, cut into 1/4-inch dice
1 yellow pepper, roasted, peeled, seeded and diced (see quesadillas page 48)

In a small bowl, combine the tuna, chives and shallots and toss to mix well. Place eight 1 1/2-inch ring molds or cans on a baking sheet which has been lined with parchment paper. Divide the ingredients so that you have enough for all 8 molds, then layer the inside of the molds in the following order, pressing down gently but firmly as you go with the back of a teaspoon or your fingers; a teaspoon of tomato cubes, salt and pepper to taste, avocado, tuna, yellow pepper, tomato, avocado, tuna. Finish with a final layer of the yellow pepper.

Assembly

Two 3-inch pieces scallion, white part only, thinly sliced on the diagonal
1 1/2 tablespoons extra virgin olive oil

Using a flat-ended metal spatula, carefully slide the spatula between the parchment paper and the bottom of the molds and lift two towers onto each of 4 large, chilled appetizer plates. Spoon a little of the tomato mousse onto each plate opposite the ahi towers.

Carefully ease the molds up and away, while holding the towers down with 2 fingers or the back of a teaspoon. Sprinkle the scallion rings around the edges of the tomato mousse and drizzle with a little of the oil.

SOMMELIER'S WINE CHOICE
Spottswoode Sauvignon Blanc (Napa Valley)
Baron de L Pouilly Fumé (Loire Valley)

"
When I have a new idea, I don't test it in advance.
I serve it as a special. I know it will taste good, even if it doesn't
satisfy my own expectations. Then I try to improve it.
If it hasn't developed right by the third time I do it, I give up on it.
"

Dungeness Crab Salad
WITH SHOESTRING POTATOES AND TWO-MUSTARD SAUCE

SERVES 4

I like the way the slightly warm and crunchy potatoes contrast with the cool and creamy salad and the sweet crab. Making shoestring potatoes is perfectly simple with a mandoline (see page 140 for a listing of mail-order sources). You could use 1 pound of lump crabmeat for this dish if you don't want to cook and crack a crab.

Crab and Potatoes

1 fresh Dungeness crab, shell on (approximately 3 pounds)
2 large Idaho potatoes
2 quarts corn or grapeseed oil

In a large saucepan, bring a generous amount of lightly salted water to a boil over high heat. Plunge the crab into the water and boil for 6 minutes, then remove it and set aside until cool enough to handle. Crack the crab using a nutcracker or a hammer, remove the crabmeat from the legs and body (do not break it up) and set aside in the refrigerator, covered, until you are ready to assemble the dish.

Peel the potatoes and use a mandoline to make shoestring potatoes. If you do not have a mandoline, cut the potatoes first into 1/4-inch-thick slices, then cut the slices into 1/4-inch-wide strips. In a large bowl, combine the shoestring potatoes with enough cold water to cover and allow to soak for 5 minutes to remove the excess starch.

In a deep fat fryer or large, heavy saucepan, heat the oil to 375 degrees F. Drain the potatoes and dry them thoroughly on kitchen towels. Fry the potatoes, stirring with tongs occasionally to keep them separated, for 9 to 10 minutes, or until golden brown. Remove with a skimmer and drain on paper towels.

Salad

1/3 cup creme fraîche
1 tablespoon Dijon mustard
1 tablespoon whole-grain mustard
1 medium shallot, finely chopped
1 tablespoon finely chopped chives
2 heads frisée (curly endive), washed and dried, with dark outer leaves discarded and pale inner
  leaves torn into bite-sized pieces
1 small carrot, cut into julienne strips
1 medium leek, white part only, cut into julienne strips
1 rib celery, strings removed, cut into julienne strips

In a medium mixing bowl, combine the crème fraîche, the 2 mustards, shallot and chives and mix together well. Add the frisée, carrot, leek and celery and toss together well, making sure that the sauce coats all the vegetables evenly.

Assembly

4 tablespoons finely chopped chives
1 tablespoon extra-virgin olive oil
1 teaspoon coarsely cracked white pepper

Reheat the shoestring potatoes in a warm oven until warmed through and crispy, then mound a quarter of them in the center of 4 large plates. Top the potatoes with a quarter of the salad, mounding it as high as you can in the center, and place 3 small piles of the crabmeat around the edge of each plate. Place 3 small mounds of chives in between each pile of crab, drizzle a touch of olive oil over the crabmeat and sprinkle the white pepper around the rim of the plate.

SOMMELIER'S WINE CHOICE
Au Bon Climat Pinot Blanc (Santa Barbara)
Bernard Chave Hermitage Blanc (Côte du Rhône)

I studied six years as an apprentice, and I dedicated myself 100 percent. If other people came to work at nine, I came at six.

Layer Cake of Odd Potato Chips
AND SMOKED STURGEON WITH HORSERADISH SAUCE

SERVES 4

This towering appetizer must be transported carefully or it could all come tumbling down! I sometimes make this dish using slices of pastrami instead of the smoked sturgeon, or you could do it with smoked salmon as well; just substitute an equal amount of either for the sturgeon. At the restaurant, the potatoes average about 1 3/4 pounds each. If you are using smaller ones, you will need two, and the potato chips will not be as long. It is really quite impossible to cut the potatoes thin enough for this dish without a mandoline or an electric slicer — they should be as thin as they can be without falling apart.

Horseradish Sauce

1 tablespoon grated fresh horseradish
1 tablespoon prepared horseradish sauce
1/2 teaspoon lemon juice
1 teaspoon finely chopped chives
1/2 cup crème fraîche
Salt and freshly ground white pepper

In a medium mixing bowl, combine all the ingredients, season to taste, set aside, cover and refrigerate.

Potato Chips

1/4 cup unsalted butter, melted
Salt and freshly ground white pepper
2 large Idaho potatoes, peeled and trimmed flat on one long edge to form a beginning
  surface for slicing

Preheat the oven to 400 degrees F. Line 2 baking sheets with parchment paper and brush with some of the butter, then sprinkle with a little salt and pepper. Using a mandoline, cut the potato blocks carefully crosswise into paper-thin ovals (you should have at least 16 slices). Lay them in a single layer on the baking sheets, brush well with the butter and sprinkle with a little more salt and pepper. Cover each layer with another sheet of parchment paper and top with another baking sheet of the same size to keep the slices flat.

Bake for 25 to 30 minutes, or until golden brown, checking to be sure the potatoes do not burn and turning the baking sheets around halfway through the cooking time to help the potatoes brown evenly. Remove the slices from the pan; if they are very oily, drain them briefly on paper towels.

Assembly

6 ounces smoked sturgeon, cut into twelve 1/4-inch slices
2 cups loosely packed mizuna salad greens, baby oak leaf lettuce or arugula leaves
2 medium shallots, finely chopped

On each of four large dinner plates, spoon a little dollop of horseradish sauce in the center of the plate and place a potato chip (the potatoes should still be lukewarm) on the top. Place a slice of the sturgeon on the potato chip, facing in the same direction, and spoon another dollop of sauce in the center of the sturgeon. Top with another potato chip at a right angle to the first chip, and continue layering in opposite directions, using 3 slices of the sturgeon and 4 potato chips for each serving. The layer cake should look like a big cross and be at least 2 1/2 inches high. Place a final dollop of the sauce in the center of the top chip and surround each of the layer cakes with 1/2 cup of the mizuna greens. Sprinkle the chopped shallots over the top of the greens.

SOMMELIER'S WINE CHOICE
Chateau Montelena Chardonnay (Napa Valley)
Dauvissat Chablis Premiere Cru "Vaillons" (Chablis)

COLD APPETIZERS

Maine Lobster Salad
WITH LEMON CRÈME FRAÎCHE, SPRING VEGETABLES AND OSETRA CAVIAR

SERVES 4

This is a light, cool and refreshing salad made extra-luxurious by the addition of a healthy mound of caviar – the amount is up to you and your wallet!
You could substitute 3/4 pound of peeled shrimp for the lobster in this salad, if desired.

Lobster

Pinch of sea salt
1/2 teaspoon red wine vinegar
One 1 1/2-pound Maine lobster, very much alive

In a large saucepan, bring a generous amount of water to a boil and add the salt and vinegar. Plunge in the lobster, cover the pan and cook for 8 minutes. Remove and drain the lobster; when it is cool enough to handle, remove the meat from the tail and claws and slice it in 1/2-inch-thick pieces. Set aside, covered, while you prepare the vegetables. Note: If it will be more than an hour until serving time, refrigerate the lobster.

Spring Vegetables

1/2 cup fresh peas
1/4 cup (2 ounces) haricots verts (very fine green beans)
2 ribs celery, cut into thick (1/4-inch) julienne strips
1/4 cup (2 ounces) baby carrots, peeled and with 1/4 inch of the green top left on
1/2 cup fresh fava beans, shelled (about 5 large pods)
3 small plum tomatoes, peeled, seeded and diced (see page 139)
1/4 cup (2 ounces) baby asparagus stalks, bottom 2 inches peeled (if using larger stalks, use only the top 3 inches and halve them lengthwise)

Have ready a large bowl of ice water. In a large saucepan, bring a generous amount of water to a boil. Using a skimmer, plunge each of the vegetables, separately, into the boiling water and blanch for 2 to 4 minutes, or until tender. Remove with the skimmer and immediately plunge each vegetable into the ice water for a minute to stop the cooking, then drain on a tea towel. Adjust the cooking time to the size and shape of the vegetables. Note: If the peas and fava beans are a similar size, they can be cooked together.

Dressing

1/2 cup crème fraîche
2 tablespoons finely chopped chives
1 teaspoon finely chopped lemon zest
1 tablespoon lemon juice

In a medium mixing bowl, combine the crème fraîche, chives, lemon zest and juice and whisk until evenly blended.

Assembly

1/2 cup oak leaf lettuce, arugula or radicchio leaves
1 to 2 ounces osetra caviar, or as much as you can afford

Add the blanched and drained vegetables and the lobster chunks to the bowl with the dressing and toss until all the ingredients are coated.

On each of four large plates, arrange a few leaves of the lettuce and mound a quarter of the lobster mixture in the center. Decorate the top with dollops of caviar.

SOMMELIER'S WINE CHOICE
Schramsberg Blanc de Blanc Sparkling Wine (Napa Valley)
Mumm Champagne "Grand Cordon" (Champagne)

COLD APPETIZERS

Terrine of Artichokes

WITH ROASTED GARLIC CLOVES AND HOLLYWOOD ROOF-DRIED TOMATOES

SERVES 12 TO 14

This terrine is strikingly beautiful but time-consuming. However, once all of the ingredients are prepared it's really a breeze to put together, and it can be out of your way completely the day before serving. When you slice across the terrine and see all the layers and cross sections of rich Mediterranean color, all that hard work will be well rewarded. It would make a perfect eye opener for a special-occasion party. Note: Once the terrine is assembled, it must rest in the refrigerator overnight to firm up before it will be ready to serve. You will have some basil-flavored oil left over for vinaigrettes and other garnishing, but it is really not worth making up in a smaller quantity.

COLD APPETIZERS

Hollywood Roof-Dried Tomatoes

(make up to 3 days in advance)
1/2 cup extra virgin olive oil
9 ripe plum tomatoes, peeled, seeded and halved lengthwise
Salt and cracked black pepper

Brush a large baking sheet with oil. Place the tomatoes, cut sides down, on the sheet and drizzle a little more oil over the top. Sprinkle with a little salt and just a touch of cracked pepper. Place the baking sheet on a Hollywood rooftop, cover with a screen and let the sun dry the tomatoes naturally, or until they are dehydrated but still a little juicy. During the summer months, when the southern California sun is at its hottest, the tomatoes will of course dry faster, but the best results will be achieved on a cloudless day after a rain, when the air is crisp and clean and you can see the Hollywood sign from miles away. (The process will take from 2 to 5 days and is a matter of taste.) Halve the tomato halves lengthwise so that you have 36 strips. Refrigerate, covered, until needed.

For those without a Hollywood rooftop, bake the tomatoes in a 250-degree -F oven for about 6 hours, or until dried but still quite juicy. These are completely unlike commercial sun-dried tomatoes and should be similar in consistency to a dried apricot that has been soaked in boiling water for half an hour. If you use commercial dry-packed sun-dried tomatoes, they should be soaked in boiling water for 30 to 40 minutes, squeezed dry and then halved lengthwise. Tomatoes packed in olive oil can simply be sliced in half before using.

Basil Oil

(make up to 1 day in advance)
1 cup firmly packed fresh basil leaves
1 cup extra virgin olive oil

Bring a small saucepan of water to the boil and blanch the basil leaves for 30 seconds. Remove them with a slotted spoon and when cool, squeeze out as much liquid as you possibly can. In a blender, combine the basil and the oil and purée for 2 to 3 minutes, or until the basil is chopped very fine. Let stand for 2 to 3 hours, then strain through a double layer of cheesecloth into a clean jar. Cover and refrigerate until needed.

Artichokes

(make 4 to 6 hours before assembling or the night before)
2 lemons, halved and juice squeezed
36 medium artichokes (about 8 ounces each), trimmed down to their bottoms (see page 139)
1 slice bacon
2 large carrots, cut into 1-inch pieces
1 large onion, cut into 1-inch pieces
4 ribs celery, cut into 1-inch pieces
1 large leek, white and light green part only, rinsed well and cut into 1-inch pieces
1 head of garlic, halved lengthwise
4 sprigs fresh thyme
2 tablespoons whole white peppercorns
1 cup white wine
3 quarts water
1 cup extra virgin olive oil

In a large mixing bowl, combine the halved lemons and their juice with a generous amount of cold water and add the artichoke bottoms and set aside.

In a large saucepan or a Dutch oven large enough to hold all the artichokes, sweat the bacon over medium-low heat for 2 to 3 minutes, or until it has rendered most of its fat. Add the carrots, onion, celery, leek, garlic, thyme and peppercorns and continue to sweat the vegetables for 10 to 12 minutes, stirring occasionally, until softened. Add the artichokes and increase the heat to medium. Sauté for 1 minute, then add the wine, water and oil. Bring the mixture to a simmer and cook for 30 to 35 minutes, or until the artichokes are tender but not falling apart. Remove from the heat and allow the artichoke bottoms to cool in the liquid until you are ready to make the artichoke mousse. *(continued on next page)*

Tomato Mousse

(make at least 4 hours before assembling)
8 plum tomatoes, peeled and seeded (see page 139)
2 tablespoons extra virgin olive oil
Salt and freshly ground white pepper

Line a colander with a double thickness of slightly dampened cheesecloth and set over a bowl. In a food processor fitted with the metal blade, process the tomatoes until completely smooth, scraping down the sides of the bowl as necessary. Place the purée in the cheesecloth-lined colander and allow it to drain for 4 hours, until very thick, and turn it out into a medium mixing bowl. Whisk the oil into the purée and season with salt and pepper to taste. Cover and set aside until you are ready to serve the terrine.

Artichoke Mousse

1 tablespoon powdered gelatin
2 tablespoons cold water
The braised artichoke bottoms and their liquid
1/2 cup extra-virgin olive oil
Salt and cayenne pepper

In a small bowl, soften the gelatin in cold water for 5 minutes, then heat over low heat for 1 minute, stirring, until smooth (do not allow to boil).

Using a slotted spoon, remove the artichokes from their braising liquid; strain the liquid, discarding the solids. Set the liquid aside. Trim each bottom into a square about 2 by 2 inches, reserving all the trimmings; return the trimmed squares to the strained braising liquid to prevent them from drying out. In a food processor fitted with the metal blade, process the artichoke trimmings for 3 to 4 minutes, or until completely smooth, scraping down the sides of the bowl as necessary. Add the oil, gelatin, salt and cayenne pepper to taste and blend again (you should have about 3 cups of mousse). For a perfectly smooth mousse, press the purée through a fine sieve into a bowl (optional).

Assembly

36 roasted cloves garlic (see page 138)

Assemble the artichoke mousse, roasted garlic cloves, sun-dried tomatoes and drained, braised artichoke squares on your work surface. Line a 1 1/2 -quart metal terrine mold or loaf pan with several pieces of plastic wrap. Press the wrap firmly into the corners and smooth it along the sides, but leave sufficient wrap overhanging so that you will have enough to seal the top. Spread a 1/2-inch-thick layer of the artichoke mousse on the bottom and sides of the mold. Arrange 12 of the artichoke squares, side by side with the hollow side up, atop the mousse, trimming them further if necessary to get them to fit into one flat layer. Place a roasted clove of garlic and a strip of sun-dried tomato inside the hollow of each one, then spread another thin layer of the artichoke mousse over the top. Create 2 more layers in the same way, then top with another 1/2-inch-thick layer of the remaining mousse. Fold the plastic wrap over the top to seal it tightly. Refrigerate the terrine overnight, or for at least 6 hours.

Serving

The reserved tomato mousse
1 cup mizuna salad or baby oak leaf lettuce
1/2 cup of the reserved basil oil
Freshly ground white pepper

Unwrap the top of the terrine and place it upside down on a piece of parchment paper. Lift the terrine or loaf pan off the top and carefully peel away the rest of the plastic wrap. Using a very sharp knife, slice the terrine into 1-inch slices and place a slice on each of 12 to 14 chilled appetizer plates. Place 4 tiny dollops of the tomato mousse around the edges of each slice and insert a small leaf of mizuna in each dollop of mousse. Drizzle the basil oil around the rim of the plate and sprinkle with a little white pepper, then serve immediately.

SOMMELIER'S WINE CHOICE
Peter Michael Chardonnay (Napa Valley)
Babcock Chardonnay "Grande Cuvée" (Santa Barbara)

Salad of Corn
SAUTÉED POTATO AND FRISÉE

SERVES 4

This salad offers a unique blend of flavors, textures and temperatures. Of course the very best time to make it is at the height of the corn season. The recipe will yield about 3/4 cup of vinaigrette and you will not need it all, so save the rest for another use. Also, it will be much easier to slice the potatoes thinly enough for this dish if you acquire a useful tool called a mandoline (see page 140 for a listing of mail-order sources).

Balsamic Vinaigrette

3 tablespoons balsamic vinegar
Salt and freshly ground white pepper
1/2 cup plus 1 tablespoon hazelnut or walnut oil

In a small bowl, whisk the vinegar with salt and pepper to taste. Add the oil in a thin stream, whisking all the time, until the mixture is emulsified. If the mixture is too thick, add a little water to thin it down, 1 teaspoonful at a time. Set aside.

Corn

2 cups fresh corn kernels (about 4 ears), or 1 pound frozen kernels, thawed
1/4 cup unsalted butter
1/2 cup milk

In a medium saucepan, combine the corn kernels with the butter and the milk and bring to a boil. Simmer until the corn is tender, about 8 to 10 minutes. Strain the corn and set it aside.

Potatoes

1/4 cup unsalted butter
2 Idaho potatoes, peeled and sliced crosswise into 1/8-inch slices
Salt and white pepper, to taste

In a large nonstick sauté pan, heat the butter over medium-high heat and sauté the potatoes in one layer (in batches if necessary). Turn and separate the potato slices occasionally to keep them from sticking together and cook for about 4 to 5 minutes, or until crisp and golden, watching carefully to see that they do not burn. Season lightly with salt and white pepper. Drain briefly on paper towels, then return all the potatoes to the pan, add the corn and stir for 1 to 2 minutes, or until completely heated through.

Assembly

2 medium shallots, finely chopped
1/3 cup finely chopped chives
2 heads frisée (curly endive), washed and dried, dark outer leaves removed and pale inner leaves cut into bite-sized pieces

In a large bowl, combine the warm corn and potato mixture with the shallots and chives and toss to mix. Just before serving, add the frisée and enough of the vinaigrette to coat the mixture and toss again until it is evenly mixed. Taste for seasoning, adjust if necessary, and serve immediately on large appetizer plates.

SOMMELIER'S WINE CHOICE
Patz and Hall Chardonnay (Napa Valley)
Cuvaison Chardonnay (Napa Valley)

COLD APPETIZERS

7:00 a.m.

When Patina's kitchen doors open, Alec Lestr, the lunch and sauce chef, is first on the scene. Two other chefs arrive just after him. "The morning's surprise," Alec announces. "The freezer went into defrost cycle during the night." Fortunately, the *chocolate confections* didn't melt.

Delivery trucks from restaurant purveyors drop off bread and dairy products, and the morning's work begins: roasting chickens, searing tuna, oven-drying tomatoes, starting the sauces. Three stockpots about the size of oil drums have been simmering stocks all night. It takes two men to pour off the stock, through a strainer, into another giant pot. The strained *broth* is placed on a large burner to reduce; it stands just outside the kitchen proper, near the walk-in refrigerators.

The kitchen is a long room with three ovens and a dozen range-top burners. These are industrial burners without built-in lighters; to light one, you turn on the gas and ignite it with the propane blowtorch used for caramelizing desserts or just toss a match in its general direction.

Up a flight of outdoor stairs is the white-tiled prep kitchen. It has two ranges of its own and an oven with a sign on it emphasizing that it's only for the use of the adjoining pastry kitchen. A six-man prep crew is already chopping *vegetables*, pitting olives, deveining shrimp and peeling asparagus. A tiny pantry at the back of the room is filled with onions, garlic, fresh ginger, *potatoes*, carrots.

Back downstairs, out in the front of the house, the restaurant's full-time carpenter is repairing the locks on the bar refrigerator. Sparks fly a foot and a half in the air as he grinds metal. Chairs have been upended on the bar to get them out of the way of the morning's vacuuming. Outside, the front windows are being cleaned. The smells of the morning: *chicken stock*, metal polish.

In the kitchen it's time to sauté the tomatoes, peppers, eggplant and zucchini for the ratatouille sauce. Two pans about the size of automobile tires are already on the range, one full of red onions and the other full of *quartered potatoes*. The vegetable chef is peeling fresh horseradish root, standing carefully upwind of it.

8:00 a.m. Fish delivery. A few minutes later a chefs calls out: "Alec, your *portobello mushrooms* are in."

The garde-manger (salad and cold-appetizer chef) is brandishing a hand blender that he's just repaired with duct tape after its fall from a shelf. "That's it," he says. "We don't keep the blender there anymore." Then he starts whipping in the *balsamic vinaigrette*. The dressing thickens almost as much as a mayonnaise – perhaps a somber, sort of intense, balsamic-colored mayonnaise.

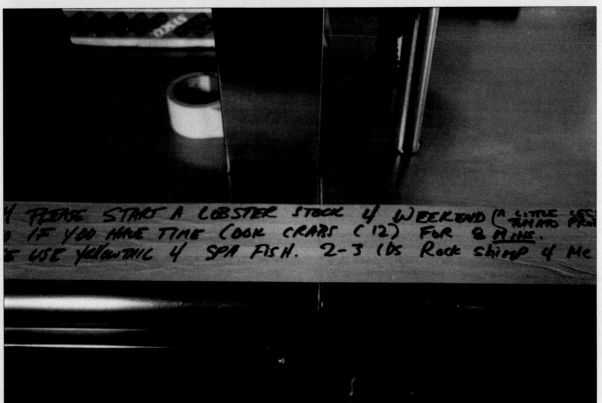

PLEASE START A LOBSTER STOCK 4 WEEKEND (A LITTLE LESS
IF YOU HAVE TIME COOK CRABS (12) FOR 8 PLINE
USE YELLOWTAIL 4 SPA FISH. 2-3 lbs ROCK SHRIMP 4 Me

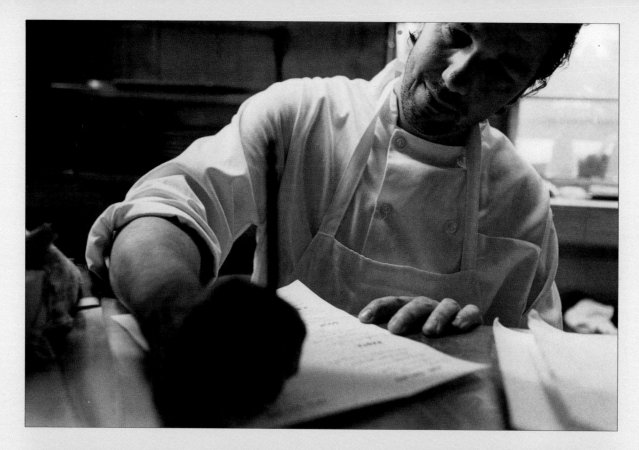

8:30 a.m.

"OK," says Alec into the phone. "So go ahead and replace the sea bass." **The fish supplier is out of the particular sea** bass variety that Patina had ordered, but has a comparable variety. "And we're still getting the *yellowtail*, right?"

The kitchen is starting to hum. The vegetable-station chef is slicing baby carrots, turnips and artichoke hearts in half for sautéing. There are plastic containers for all the vegetables, including the baby turnips, chopped celery, *roasted tomatoes*, green beans and yellow wax beans. Behind him is a rack of fried basil leaves and truffle chips for the vegetarian special.

Large artichoke hearts float in a 12-quart pot of simmering water. A *vegetable* mixture called mirepoix is sautéing in two huge saucepans. Housemade stock, frozen into the size of shoeboxes - is being melted in other pans. The garde-manger, who works away from the ranges at the far end of the kitchen, is methodically separating endives, making a big green-and-white heap of leaves.

"Is 50 blinis a reasonable number to make for dinner?" asks the hot-appetizer chef. "No." says Alec. "We're gonna do at least 150 covers tonight. Better do more blinis to be safe."

9:45 a.m.

Another chef clocks in, and a waitress. Executive chef Jonny Fernow comes in. **"Jonny Inferno!"** Alec calls out gennially.

"What's going on?" Jonny asks, glancing through some papers. "Is the Hollywood Bowl busy? Sauces OK? The dinner OK? Turkey breasts come in? Lobster stock made for the *nage* last night?"

A hostess comes in to talk to Jonny. "There's a guy on the phone. He's a little upset that **Joachim** isn't going to be here on the day he's coming; he sounds serious about it."

"Ask him whether he wants to reschedule."

Alec and Jonny compare notes on apron stains. "I tried the bleach and they came out spotlessly clean," Jonny says. "You leave 'em a long time on low setting."

The mirepoix mixture is done, and now the meat chef is searing a *veal shank* for dinner. It will be roasted with the mirepoix, then, after lunch, it will go into the oven to braise through the afternoon.

The hot-appetizer chef, wearing a baseball cap backwards, is caramelizing *shallots* for the pasta special, *bucatini* with shallots, garlic, anchovies and crisp-fried capers and olives. "I'd like to get married," he muses, scraping the bottom of the pan with a spatula. "It gives you something to do when you get off work."

The pastry station is located in a cool corner of the kitchen. Posted on the wall, near the list of emergency numbers, is a checkoff list of things for the pastry chef to do during the daytime:

Things for the pastry chef to do:

Crème brûlées *(ramekins cleaned off)*

Bake off banana tarts

Prebake orange tarts

Tuile cups

Taboule *(assemble)*

Cut fruit for taboule

Unmold vanilla timbales

Berry compote

Apricot bavarians *(cut and bake off puff bottoms, apricot wafers)*

Rhubarb cooked *(pick strawberries 1/4ed for poppyseed dumplings)*

Sabayon *(peach and rhubarb plate)*

Peaches in tins *(puff bottoms)*

Berry plate

Cookies *(assorted)*

Macaroons *(pipe)*

Poppyseed dumplings

Sorbets: *vanilla, coffee, hazelnut, almond, chocolate, mango lime, banana, apricot*

Sauces: *vanilla, chocolate, praline, passion fruit, mango, raspberry, strawberry coulis*

Things to do when not busy:

Cut plastic for crunchy cakes

Zest orange for candying

Peel rhubarb

Pit cherries

Scoop cookie dough

Chop chocolate

Roll filling for dumplings

Fill clean sauce bottles

Clean tart mats

10:00 a.m.

A boombox fills the kitchen with rock music all morning. As the chefs work they gripe about the radio station's predictable programming: always the same musicians at the same time of day. "If this is Ozzy," says Jonny, sonorously summing up, "it must be asparagus."

Trays of *roasted chickens* come out of the oven. The hot-appetizer chef tears up bunches of basil for a pesto sauce. *Corn kernels* poach in a 20-quart stockpot. Chop, chop, chop, chop.

Jonny gets off the phone and alerts the kitchen to a big lunch reservation. "We've got a 10-top at 12 that has to be out at 1," he says, "and they're ordering à la carte." Well, at least it's nice to know ahead of time that you're going to have 10 people all ordering different things that will have to be served at the same moment. Unlike dinner, lunch isn't usually booked up in advance, and the kitchen has only a general idea of how much it will be cooking.

Only one thing is certain about lunch: In hot weather, fish and salad are going to fly. Today they can expect to serve a lot of *spa lunches* (salad and fish of the day), as well as the other prix-fixe menu, the American business lunch (salad and pasta of the day).

"I want bacon fired up," calls Alec. "Do we have *Swiss cheese* in the house?" No. He writes a note to himself on a piece of freezer tape, using a felt-tip marker, and posts it on a pillar at his work station.

Three oversized trays come out of the oven. *Bacon's* on one. The second is a tray of browned pine nuts. On the third are the pastry buns that Patina uses in its whimsical interpretation of a BLT. Alec peers at a pot and taps it with a ladle. "Is this just simmering?" he asks a chef. "I want it to boil down as fast as possible." A waiter sticks his head in the kitchen to report the latest development in a televised sports event.

Out front, **the restaurant is being readied for lunch**. The day's newspapers are being laid out on the bar. The chairs that were stowed on the bar during vacuuming are on the floor again. Freshly laundered cloths are going on the tables, and the waiters are brushing crumbs from the seats in the booths. Fans are blowing to rid the room of cleaning odors, particularly the smell of metal polish.

11:00 a.m. The staff eats the lunch they've made for themselves as they worked through the morning. It's pasta with the vegetable chef's own interpretation of *pesto sauce* made from roasted, rather than raw, garlic and spiked with plumped yellow raisins.

Santa Barbara Shrimp

WITH MASHED POTATOES AND POTATO TRUFFLE CHIPS

SERVES 4

This is one of our most popular dishes at Patina, containing both my signature ingredients: spuds and truffles. (In the absence of truffles, you could make the truffle chips with flat Italian parsley leaves.) Again, you will need a mandoline to slice the potatoes thin enough for this dish. They should be as thin as they can possibly be without falling apart.

Potato Truffle Chips

1/4 cup unsalted butter, melted
Salt and freshly ground white pepper
1 large Idaho potato, peeled

1/4 ounce black truffle, thinly sliced
and trimmed into 1/4-inch squares
Salt and freshly ground pepper

Preheat the oven to 375 degrees F. Line a baking sheet with parchment paper, brush it with some of the butter, then sprinkle with a little salt and pepper. Using a mandoline, slice the potatoes crosswise into paper-thin slices (you must have at least 24 slices) and arrange 12 of the potato circles in a single layer on paper. Brush the potatoes with butter and sprinkle with a little more salt and pepper. Place a truffle square on each potato circle, then cover with another potato circle to create 12 "truffle sandwiches." Brush the tops with butter, cover with another sheet of parchment paper and top with another baking sheet to weight them down. Bake for about 35 to 40 minutes, until evenly golden, checking to be sure the potatoes do not burn and turning the sheet around halfway through the cooking time to help the potatoes to brown evenly. Sprinkle with salt and pepper. Set the chips aside on a baking sheet lined with paper towels until you are ready to assemble the dish.

Fried Leeks

1 cup corn oil
1 large leek, green part only, rinsed thoroughly and cut into thin julienne strips

In a large, heavy saucepan, heat the corn oil to 350 degrees F. Pat the leek strips with paper towels until completely dry, then, using a skimmer, place them in the hot oil and cook for about 2 to 3 minutes, stirring once, until they are crisp. Drain on paper towels and mound them on the baking sheet alongside the truffle chips.

SOMMELIER'S WINE CHOICE
El Molino Chardonnay (Napa Valley)
Domaine de Comtes Lafon Meursault "Clos de la Barre"
(White Burgundy, Côte de Beaune)

Mashed Potatoes

3 cups milk
2 medium Idaho potatoes, peeled
and quartered

1/2 cup unsalted butter
1/4 cup heavy cream
Salt and freshly ground white pepper

In a large saucepan, combine the milk and the potatoes and bring to a boil. Reduce the heat and simmer the potatoes for about 20 to 25 minutes, until tender. Drain the potatoes and pass them through a food mill or mash thoroughly with a hand blender or potato masher (do not use a food processor).

Place the potatoes in a clean pan. In a small saucepan, bring the butter and cream to a boil. Slowly add the cream mixture to the mashed potatoes, stirring all the time, over low heat. Season to taste with salt and pepper and remove from the heat. Cover and set aside.

Shrimp

2 tablespoons clarified butter (see page 136)
12 Santa Barbara or other very large shrimp (16/20 count), peeled and deveined (see page 139)

In a large sauté pan, heat the clarified butter over high heat and sauté the shrimp for 1 to 2 minutes on each side, or until just done through.

Assembly

2/3 cup lobster nage, warm (see page 137)

Preheat the oven to 300 degrees F. Reheat the truffle chips and fried leeks in the oven until just warmed through. In 4 heated, large soup bowls, mound equal portions of the mashed potatoes. Arrange 3 shrimp around each mound and spoon some of the lobster nage around. Place 3 truffle chips upright in the potatoes and make a little nest of the leeks in the center.

Potato Cannelloni
WITH CONFIT OF DUCK AND ROASTED SHIITAKES

SERVES 4

It is possible to buy duck confit from some gourmet supply stores and mail-order catalogues (see page 140), but you can make it yourself if you purchase or save up enough rendered duck or chicken fat from previous dishes. At the restaurant we use only Mallard ducks, but you could make this with any nice large duck. The fat can be used again after making the confit; it is wonderful for sautéing potatoes! Freeze the remaining confit for another use.

(see page 140)

Duck Confit

(make the night before)

2 duck legs and thigh joints,
    about 12 ounces each
1/4 cup kosher salt
1 bunch fresh thyme

4 cloves garlic, unpeeled but
    slightly crushed with a chef's knife
1/2 teaspoon whole white peppercorns
3 cups rendered duck or chicken fat

The night before: Line a baking sheet with parchment paper and set the duck pieces on it. Sprinkle the salt evenly over the duck and arrange the thyme, garlic and peppercorns over the top. Seal tightly with plastic wrap and refrigerate overnight.

The next day: Preheat the oven to 250 degrees F. Wipe the salt from the duck pieces and place them in a casserole just large enough to hold them. Add the duck fat, which must cover all the pieces, and bake uncovered for about 2 1/2 hours, or until the meat is falling off the bones. Remove the duck pieces from the fat, and when cool enough to handle, shred the meat and reserve. Discard the skin, bones and fat, but reserve 1/4 cup of the fat for the final assembly.

Filling for Cannelloni

2 tablespoons extra virgin olive oil
1/2 small carrot, cut into 1/4-inch dice
2 medium shallots, cut into 1/4-inch dice
1/2 rib celery, strings removed and
    cut into 1/4-inch dice

1/2 small leek, white part only,
    cut into 1/4-inch dice
1 tablespoon dry white wine
1 cup of the reserved duck confit
1 tablespoon finely chopped Italian
    (flat-leaf) parsley

In a large sauté pan, heat the oil over medium heat. Add the vegetables and cook, stirring occasionally, for 4 to 5 minutes, or until softened. Do not allow them to brown. Add the wine and stir to mix thoroughly, then add the duck confit and the parsley and remove from the heat. Set aside.

Potato Cannelloni

1/4 cup unsalted butter, melted
Salt and freshly ground white pepper

2 large Idaho potatoes, peeled and trimmed
    flat on one long edge to form a beginning
    surface for slicing

Preheat the oven to 350 degrees F. Line 2 baking sheets with parchment paper and brush with some of the butter, then sprinkle with a little salt and pepper. With a mandoline or a sharp knife, cut the potatoes carefully lengthwise into 1/8-inch-thick oval slices (you should have at least 24 slices) and arrange them in a single layer on the baking sheets. Brush the slices well with the butter and sprinkle with a little more salt and pepper. Cover with another sheet of parchment paper and bake for 10 to 12 minutes, or until fork-tender. Set aside, on the baking sheets, until cool enough to handle.

Lay an 8-inch-long sheet of plastic wrap on the work surface. By slightly overlapping 2 slices of potato parallel in the center of the plastic, create a 3-inch by 6-inch sheet of potatoes with rounded edges. Place 2 to 3 teaspoons of the duck filling on one short edge of the sheet and roll it up tightly, using the plastic wrap to help roll, and seal the plastic tightly. Repeat the process to make another 11 rolls and refrigerate them for 1 to 2 hours to firm.

Assembly

2 tablespoons unsalted butter
12 small shiitake mushroom caps
2 medium shallots, finely chopped
4 cups (1/4 pound) spinach leaves,
    washed, dried and stems removed
2 teaspoons reserved duck fat or clarified butter
    (see page 136)

3/4 cup reduced duck stock (see page 136)
2 tablespoons unsalted butter, at room
    temperature, for the sauce
1 teaspoon finely chopped Italian
    (flat-leaf) parsley
Salt and freshly ground white pepper

In a small sauté pan, melt 1 tablespoon of the butter over medium-high heat and sauté the mushrooms for 4 to 5 minutes, turning halfway through the cooking time until crisp outside and tender inside. Set aside.

In a medium sauté pan, melt the remaining 1 tablespoon of butter over medium heat. Add the shallots and cook for 2 to 3 minutes, or until slightly softened. Add the spinach leaves and cook just until wilted, tossing occasionally, about 1 1/2 minutes. Set aside.

Remove the potato cannelloni from the plastic wrap and place on a work surface near the stove. In a large nonstick skillet, heat the reserved fat over medium heat and sauté the cannelloni, using tongs to turn them carefully until they are golden on all sides. You will probably need to do this in batches. Bring the reduced duck stock to a simmer and swirl in the butter, stirring and swirling just until emulsified. Remove from the heat and stir in the parsley, mushrooms and salt and pepper to taste. Divide the spinach among 4 heated serving bowls and place 3 cannelloni in each one. Spoon the duck sauce over the top, making sure to give each bowl 3 shiitake caps.

SOMMELIER'S WINE CHOICE
Calera Pinot Noir "Jensen" (Central Coast) Hitching Post Pinot Noir (Santa Barbara)

Roasted Chicken Wings
WITH UNORTHODOX CHOPPED LIVER

SERVES 4

I wanted to challenge the best delicatessen chopped liver in town with this refined dish, which, incidentally, glorifies another humble ingredient – chicken wings!

Chicken Wings

24 pieces of the middle bone portion of chicken wings (reserve other parts for making stock)
Salt and freshly ground white pepper
1/4 cup unsalted butter
2 cloves garlic, unpeeled
1 sprig fresh thyme

Standing a chicken wing on end, use a sharp knife to scrape and push the meat down around the end and bunch it up, creating a "minidrumstick". Remove the extra small bone that is exposed in the process. Repeat with the remaining wing bones and season the drumsticks with salt and pepper.

In a large sauté pan, melt the butter over medium-high heat and add the garlic cloves and thyme. In batches if necessary, sauté the wings for 3 to 4 minutes, or until golden brown and crispy, turning with tongs to brown all sides evenly. Reduce the heat to low and finish cooking the wings for 8 to 10 minutes, or until done through with no trace of pink remaining. Drain briefly on paper towels and set aside, covered with aluminum foil. Pour off the fat from the sauté pan, reserving the garlic and thyme, and make the sauce in the same pan.

Sauce

1 tablespoon unsalted butter
1 small carrot, cut into 1/4-inch dice
1/4 small yellow onion, cut into 1/4-inch dice
2 tablespoons dry white wine
1 1/2 cups chicken stock (see page 136)
1/4 cup unsalted butter at room temperature, cut into 2 pieces
1 tablespoon finely chopped Italian (flat-leaf) parsley
Salt and freshly ground white pepper

Return the sauté pan to medium heat and add the butter. Add the carrot, onion, reserved garlic cloves and thyme and cook for 3 to 4 minutes, or until the vegetables have softened. Add the wine and deglaze the pan, stirring and scraping the bottom and sides to release all of the flavorful bits into the liquid, and continue to cook until the wine has almost completely evaporated. Add the stock and simmer, stirring occasionally, until reduced by about half, with about 3/4 cup of liquid remaining. Remove and discard

the whole garlic and thyme. Reduce the heat and swirl in the butter a piece at a time, just until emulsified, then remove from the heat and add the parsley and salt and pepper to taste. Set aside, covered, until you are ready to assemble the dish.

Chopped Liver Croutons

10 ounces chicken livers
Salt and freshly ground white pepper
1/4 cup unsalted butter at room temperature
2 medium shallots, finely chopped
1 tablespoon finely chopped chives
2 ounces fresh "A" grade duck liver, cut into 1/4-inch cubes
8 thin oval slices country-style white bread, toasted until golden brown

Preheat the oven to 300 degrees F. Season the chicken livers with salt and pepper. In a medium sauté pan, over medium-high heat, melt half the butter and cook the livers for 3 to 4 minutes, turning with tongs until they are evenly browned on the outside but still pink on the inside. Remove the livers to a cutting board and chop coarsely. Combine the liver in a medium bowl with the remaining butter (cut into small pieces so that it will make a creamy binder), shallots, chives and the cubed duck liver; toss gently just to mix well. Mound some of the "chopped liver" on one side of each crouton and return to the warm oven on a baking sheet for 1 to 2 minutes, or until just heated through (the duck liver will begin to "melt" as soon as it is warm).

Assembly

Gently reheat the sauce over low heat and return the chicken wings to the hot oven for 2 minutes, or until heated through. In each of 4 heated soup plates, place 2 croutons end-to-end across the center, bisecting it, with the liver-mounded sides closest to the center. Fan 3 drumsticks on the plate above the croutons with the meat toward the center and fan 3 more on the plate below the croutons. Spoon some of the sauce over all.

SOMMELIER'S WINE CHOICE
Williams Selyem Pinot Noir (Russian River)
Mongeard-Mugneret Givry (Red Burgundy, Mercurey)

37

Sculpin

SERVES 4

This not very beautiful relative of the rockfish is rarely marketed commercially in America, but in France, as the noble "rascasse," it is an essential ingredient of bouillabaisse. Cleaning sculpin requires care, (see page 139) so ask your fish monger to prepare them for you. If you can't find sculpin, you can substitute red snapper, which has a similar white flesh and is easier to handle.

Plum Tomato Sauce

1/4 cup plus 2 tablespoons extra virgin olive oil
2 medium shallots, finely chopped
8 plum tomatoes, peeled, seeded and quartered (see page 139)
2 cloves garlic, crushed with the side of a chef's knife
1 sprig of thyme

In a medium sauté pan, heat 1/4 cup of the oil over medium-low heat. Add the shallots and sauté for 3 to 4 minutes, or until softened. Add the tomatoes, garlic and thyme, increase the heat to medium and continue to cook for 8 to 10 minutes, or until the tomatoes have begun to break down. The mixture will still be chunky and quite wet. Remove the garlic and thyme, stir in the 2 tablespoons of oil and remove the pan from the heat. Set aside, covered.

Zucchini Mousse

3 slices white bread, crusts removed and torn into small pieces
3 tablespoons heavy cream
1 tablespoon extra virgin olive oil
3 medium zucchini, skin and outermost 1/2 inch of flesh removed in strips all the way around, center core discarded, blanched for 1 minute in boiling water and drained
Salt and freshly ground white pepper
5 leaves fresh basil

In a small mixing bowl, combine the bread with the cream and toss to mix. In a medium sauté pan, heat the oil over medium heat. Add the zucchini and sauté for 2 to 3 minutes, or until softened. Salt and pepper the zucchini and drain briefly on paper towels to remove some of the moisture. In a food processor fitted with the metal blade, combine the bread mixture, zucchini and basil. Process for 10 to 20 seconds, scraping down the sides of the bowl as necessary. Set aside.

Sculpin

2 teaspoons extra virgin olive oil
4 sculpin, about 8 to 10 ounces each, prepared as directed on page 139 (or use rockfish or red snapper, gutted through the backbone, belly left intact)
1/4 cup fresh white bread crumbs, ground very fine

Preheat the oven to 350 degrees F. Brush the bottom of a roasting pan large enough to hold all the fish with the oil. Rinse the fish, set them right side up in the pan and open out the sides of each fish to form a surface for the zucchini mousse. Spread the mousse evenly over the inside surface of the fish and roast in the oven for 8 to 10 minutes, or until firm. Remove the pan from the oven and sprinkle the bread crumbs evenly over the mousse. Place the pan under a hot broiler for 2 to 3 minutes, or until the bread crumbs are golden.

Assembly

1 tablespoon basil chiffonade (see page 139)

Gently reheat the tomato sauce in its pan and stir in the basil. On each of 4 heated appetizer plates, make a pool of the sauce. Using a spatula and kitchen tongs to lift the fish, place one sculpin over the sauce on each plate.

SOMMELIER'S WINE CHOICE
Ferrari-Carrano Chardonnay (Napa Valley)
Rombauer Chardonnay (Napa Valley)

Roasted Artichokes
WITH LARGE SEA SCALLOPS, SUMMER TRUFFLES AND MIZUNA

SERVES 4

This dish was created specifically for the summer truffle season.
The earthy tang of the truffles creates an ideal balance with the sweetness of the scallops.

Artichokes

1 lemon, halved and juice squeezed
4 large artichokes (about 12 ounces each), stems left on, tough outer leaves snapped off, top
*   two -thirds of the leaves cut off and stems and bases peeled to remove the tough fibers*
1 slice bacon
1 large carrot, cut into 1-inch pieces
1 small onion, cut into 1-inch pieces
1 rib celery, cut into 1-inch pieces
1 large leek, white and light green part only, well rinsed and cut into 1-inch pieces
1/2 head of unpeeled garlic, halved lengthwise
2 sprigs fresh thyme
2 teaspoons whole white peppercorns
1/2 cup white wine
1 quart water
1/4 cup extra virgin olive oil

In a large mixing bowl, combine the lemon halves and juice with a generous amount of cold water and add the artichokes as you trim them.

In a large saucepan, sweat the bacon over medium-low heat for 2 to 3 minutes, or until it has rendered its fat. Add the carrot, onion, celery, leek, garlic, thyme and peppercorns and continue to sweat the vegetables for 8 to 10 minutes, or until softened. Add the artichokes and increase the heat to medium. Sauté for 1 minute, then add the wine, water and oil. Bring the mixture to a simmer and cook for 20 to 25 minutes, or until the artichokes are just tender but not mushy. Remove from the heat and leave them in the braising liquid until cool enough to handle. Halve them vertically and remove the chokes. Set aside until you are ready for the final assembly.

Sauce

2 tablespoons truffle jus (see page 139)
2 tablespoons extra virgin olive oil
1 ounce fresh or canned black truffle, thinly sliced
1 tablespoon finely chopped Italian (flat-leaf) parsley
Freshly ground white pepper

In a small saucepan over medium-high heat, bring the truffle jus and oil to a simmer. Remove from the heat and add the sliced truffle. Allow to infuse for 5 minutes, then stir in the parsley and season to taste with freshly ground pepper (the truffle jus will have enough salt). Set aside, covered.

Scallops

12 large sea scallops (about 1 1/2 ounces each)
Salt and freshly ground white pepper
1 tablespoon extra virgin olive oil

Season the scallops with salt and pepper. In a medium sauté pan, heat the oil over medium-high heat until very hot. Sauté the scallops for 1 to 2 minutes on each side, or until browned outside and medium-rare inside (do not overcook or they will become rubbery). Drain briefly on paper towels and keep covered while you finish the dish.

Assembly

1 tablespoon unsalted butter
4 cups mizuna greens, arugula, baby oak leaf or other salad greens
Sea salt

Preheat the oven to 400 degrees F. In a large, ovenproof sauté pan, melt the butter over medium heat. Add the artichoke halves, cut side down, and sauté for 3 to 4 minutes, or until golden. Turn to the other side and finish cooking in the hot oven for 5 minutes more. Gently reheat the truffle sauce, but do not allow it to boil.

On each of 4 heated large dinner plates, mound a quarter of the greens. Place an artichoke half in the center and lean another half upright against it. Position 3 warm scallops around the plate at twelve, five and seven o'clock and drizzle some truffle sauce over them. Drizzle a bit over the artichokes as well and sprinkle just a touch of sea salt over all.

SOMMELIER'S WINE CHOICE
Sinskey Chardonnay "Aries" (Napa Valley)
MacRostie Chardonnay (Napa Valley)

Potato Oyster Ravioli
WITH AGED ZINFANDEL SAUCE

SERVES 4

This recipe is one of the reasons I am sometimes called "The Potato Meister." It gives me pleasure to use the humble potato instead of pasta to create a dish that is at once sophisticated, beautiful and delicious.

Ravioli

1/3 cup (3 ounces) unsalted butter, melted

Salt and freshly ground white pepper

2 large Idaho potatoes, peeled and trimmed flat on one small end to form a beginning
  surface for slicing

24 medium Malpeque oysters, or other oysters such as Kumamoto or Fanny Bay

2 medium shallots, finely chopped

1 teaspoon finely chopped chives

Preheat the oven to 350 degrees F. Line 2 baking sheets with parchment paper and brush with some of the butter, then sprinkle with a little salt and pepper. With a mandoline or a sharp knife, slice the potatoes crosswise into paper-thin ovals (you should have at least 24 slices). Arrange them in a single layer on the baking sheets, brush well with the butter and sprinkle with a little more salt and pepper. Cover with another sheet of parchment paper and bake for 10 to 12 minutes, or until fork-tender. Do not allow to brown.

Remove the top layer of parchment paper and, when the potato slices are cool enough to handle, place an oyster on one side of each slice, sprinkle a few shallots and chives over each and fold the other side of the slice over to form a half-moon-shaped ravioli. Press the edges very gently together (the butter will help them to stay closed), then set the ravioli on the baking sheet. Set aside, covered with a tea towel, until you are ready to finish the dish (not more than 1 hour).

Shallot Garnish

Vegetable oil for deep-frying

1/2 cup all-purpose flour

Salt and freshly ground white pepper

8 large shallots, very thinly sliced and then separated into rings

In a large, heavy saucepan or deep-fryer, heat the oil to 350 degrees F. On a large dinner plate, toss together the flour and salt and pepper to taste. Dredge the rings in the seasoned flour, shaking off any excess flour. Using a skimmer, plunge the shallot rings into the hot oil and fry until crispy and golden, about 3 to 4 minutes. Remove and drain on a baking sheet lined with paper towels.

Zinfandel Sauce

2 tablespoons unsalted butter

4 medium shallots, finely chopped

1 1/2 cups good, aged Zinfandel wine

1/2 cup chicken stock (see page 136)

1/2 cup unsalted butter at room temperature, cut into 4 pieces

1 teaspoon finely chopped chives

In a medium sauté pan over medium heat, melt the butter and cook the shallots, stirring, for 3 to 4 minutes, or until softened. Add the wine and the stock and increase the heat to medium-high. Bring the liquid to a low boil and reduce until syrupy, with only about 1/2 cup remaining. Reduce the heat to low and swirl in the butter, a piece at a time, stirring constantly and adding the next piece when the last one is almost absorbed. Remove the pan from the heat and stir in the chives.

Assembly

Preheat the oven to 300 degrees F. Reheat the shallot rings and warm the ravioli for just a few minutes, or until the potato wrapper is warm but the oyster inside is just lukewarm. In each of 4 heated, large soup bowls, carefully arrange 6 ravioli in a circle with the rounded sides facing out, leaving a space in the middle. (You will have to be very careful in transferring the ravioli so that the oyster doesn't fall out —the edges are not really sealed). Drizzle some of the sauce over the ravioli and place some of the fried shallots in the center of the bowl.

SOMMELIER'S WINE CHOICE
Storybook Mountain Zinfandel (Napa Valley)
Rocking Horse Zinfandel (Napa Valley)

Maine Lobster "Harahan"

WITH WHITE BEAN MOUSSE AND HAM HOCKS

SERVES 4

I created this dish for one of our good customers, Michael Harahan. It is a favorite of mine because it combines luxurious food with peasant fare.

Soaking the Beans

(do at least 6 hours ahead)
3/4 cup dried white beans, such as navy or great Northern

Place the dried beans in a large bowl, cover with cold water to a depth of 2 inches and allow to soak for 6 hours or overnight.

Ham Hock

1 smoked ham hock
2 cups chicken stock (see page 136)
1 small carrot, coarsely chopped

1/4 small yellow onion, coarsely chopped
1 clove garlic, halved
1 bay leaf

Preheat the oven to 325 degrees F. In a small roasting pan, combine the ham hock with the other ingredients. Cover with aluminum foil and roast for 1 to 1 1/2 hours, or until the meat is fairly tender, turning the hock over halfway through the cooking time. Remove from the oven, and when cool enough to handle, remove the skin and discard the fat. Cut the skin into julienne strips and separate the meat into chunks approximately 1/2 inch thick. Set both aside, covered, until the final assembly. Strain and reserve the liquid, discarding the solids. There should be about 2 cups.

White Bean Mousse

1 1/2 quarts chicken stock
The reserved liquid from the ham hock
1 medium carrot
1 rib celery

1/2 medium yellow onion
1/2 clove garlic
1 sprig fresh thyme
Salt and freshly ground white pepper

Drain the soaked beans. In a large saucepan, combine them with the chicken stock, ham cooking liquid, carrot, celery, onion, garlic and thyme and bring to a simmer over medium heat. Reduce the heat and simmer for 30 minutes, then season to taste with salt and pepper. Simmer for 30 minutes more, or until the beans are very tender and falling apart. Remove and discard the vegetables. Drain the beans, reserving the stock, and purée them in a food processor fitted with the metal blade or a blender, pulsing on and off and scraping down the sides of the bowl as necessary. You may have to add up to 1/4 cup of the reserved stock to make the bean mousse move in the processor, but it should remain dry enough to hold its shape well and not be at all soupy. Turn the mousse into a saucepan and set aside, covered, until you are ready to finish the dish.

Lobster

Sea salt
1 teaspoon red wine vinegar

Two 1 1/2-pound Maine lobsters, very much alive

In a very large saucepan, bring a generous amount of water to a boil and add a touch of salt and the vinegar. Plunge in the lobsters, cover the pan, and cook for 6 minutes, then remove them and drain. When they are cool enough to handle, remove the meat from the tails and claws and slice it in 1/2 -inch-thick pieces.

Assembly

1/2 cup lobster stock (see page 137)
1/4 cup unsalted butter, at room temperature, cut into 2 pieces, for the sauce
Salt and freshly ground white pepper
1 tablespoon finely chopped Italian (flat-leaf) parsley
2 tablespoons unsalted butter, for the mousse

In a small saucepan over high heat, reduce the lobster stock by half, then lower the heat to a simmer and swirl in the butter, a piece at a time, until evenly mixed and slightly thickened. Add the ham, skin and lobster meat and salt and pepper to taste. Stir together for 2 minutes, or just until heated through, then remove from the heat and stir in the parsley. Gently reheat the bean mousse and stir in the butter. (The mixture should be very thick, but if it is too thick, thin it with a little of the reserved bean stock.) Mound some of the mousse into each of 4 heated serving bowls and spoon over some of the sauce, making sure each diner gets an equal amount of ham and lobster.

SOMMELIER'S WINE CHOICE
Jade Mountain Syrah (Napa Valley)
Jaboulet Hermitage "La Chapelle" (Côtes du Rhône)

Potato and Forest Mushroom Lasagna
WITH CHIVE SAUCE

SERVES 4

I think this dish can challenge any lasagna made from conventional pasta, and the technique of making tender potato sheets is really quite easily mastered once you have done it two or three times. The recipe calls for four different types of mushrooms, but in a pinch you could use 3/4 pound of one kind of mushroom, although, of course the flavor will not be as rich. You could cook the potato layers earlier in the day and leave them, covered with the parchment paper, until just before assembling the dish.

HOT APPETIZERS

Potatoes

1/4 cup unsalted butter, melted
Salt and freshly ground white pepper
2 large Idaho potatoes, peeled and trimmed into approximately 3-inch by 2-inch blocks
  (reserve the trimmings in a bowl of cold water to make mashed potatoes, if desired)

Preheat an oven to 350 degrees F. Line 2 baking sheets with parchment paper and brush them with some of the melted butter. Sprinkle with a little salt and pepper onto the paper. With a mandoline or a sharp knife, cut the potato blocks carefully crosswise into 1/8-inch-thick rectangles (each potato should yield 9 to 10 slices) and arrange them in a single layer on the baking sheets. Brush the slices well with the butter and sprinkle with a little more salt and pepper. Cover with another sheet of parchment paper and bake for 12 to 15 minutes, or until fork-tender. Set aside, on the baking sheets.

Mushrooms

1/4 cup unsalted butter
1 1/4 cups thinly sliced white mushrooms, stems removed
1 1/4 cups thinly sliced shiitake mushrooms, stems removed
1 1/4 cups thinly sliced oyster mushrooms, stems removed
1 1/4 cups thinly sliced chanterelle or porcini mushrooms, if available
1 large shallot, finely chopped
1 tablespoon finely chopped chives
Salt and freshly ground white pepper

In a large sauté pan, melt the butter over medium-high heat. When the foam has subsided and it is just beginning to turn brown, add the white mushrooms and sauté, stirring, for 1 minute; then add the shiitakes and stir for another minute; finally add the oysters and chanterelles, if using. Cook the mushrooms until all their liquid has evaporated, about 5 to 6 minutes more. Add the shallot and the chives, stir to mix well, season to taste with salt and white pepper and remove from the heat.

On a baking sheet, make 4 individual lasagne by layering first a single sheet of potato, then a nice thick layer of the mushroom mixture, then another sheet of potato, and so on. Use 4 potato layers in all and 3 layers of mushroom mixture and end with a potato layer. Place the other baking sheet on top of the lasagne with a weight on it and allow the lasagne to compress for 1 hour, otherwise they will tend to fall apart.

Chive Sauce and Assembly

1 1/4 cups vegetable nage (see page 137)
1 tablespoon finely chopped chives
1 medium plum tomato, peeled, seeded and diced (see page 139)

Half an hour before serving, preheat the oven to 350 degrees F. Bring the vegetable nage to a simmer. Stir in the chives and diced tomato.

Place the lasagne in the oven and reheat until they are warmed through, about 4 to 6 minutes. Using a flat-ended metal spatula, transfer the lasagne to individual heated appetizer plates. Spoon a little of the sauce over and around each one.

SOMMELIER'S WINE CHOICE
Robert Mondavi Pinot Noir "Reserve" (Napa Valley)
Etude Pinot Noir (Napa Valley)

Santa Barbara Shrimp

WITH BRIGHT YELLOW POLENTA, PANCETTA, ASPARAGUS TIPS AND SHRIMP TARRAGON JUS

SERVES 4

Pancetta is a raw, unsmoked Italian bacon, completely different from American bacon and Italian prosciutto. It is available at most Italian delis and specialty stores. It is very difficult to slice thinly, so have the deli do it for you.

HOT APPETIZERS

Shrimp Tarragon Jus

12 Santa Barbara shrimp (or other large
fresh shrimp), shells on
3 tablespoons extra virgin olive oil
1 tablespoon cognac
1 cup dry white wine
2 medium shallots, finely chopped
1 sprig fresh tarragon

1 sprig fresh thyme
2 cloves garlic, halved
1 tablespoon tomato paste
1 to 1 1/4 quarts
lobster stock (see page 137)
Salt and freshly ground white pepper

Preheat the oven to 400 degrees F. Peel and devein the shrimp (see page 139) and refrigerate them, covered, until ready to assemble the dish. Place the shells in a large roasting pan and drizzle with 2 tablespoons of the oil. Roast them for 15 to 20 minutes, stirring once or twice, until they are bright red and beginning to caramelize. Remove the pan from the oven and add the cognac and wine. Deglaze the pan, stirring and scraping the bottom and sides to release all the flavorful bits into the liquid; set aside. Reduce the oven temperature to 300 degrees F for crisping the pancetta.

In a large heavy saucepan, heat the remaining tablespoon of oil over medium heat. Add the shallots and sauté, stirring occasionally, for 3 to 4 minutes, or until softened. Add the roasted shells with their deglazing liquid, the tarragon, thyme and garlic and stir for 5 minutes. Add the tomato paste and cook, stirring, for a further 2 minutes, then add the lobster stock, adding water if necessary to cover the shells by 1 inch. Bring the liquid to a boil, then reduce the heat and simmer for 1 hour, skimming off fats and impurities as needed.

While the stock is simmering, cook the pancetta (see instructions below). Strain the liquid through a strainer lined with a double thickness of slightly dampened cheesecloth into a small saucepan, pressing down on the solids to extract all their flavor. Discard the solids. Over medium-high heat, reduce the stock by about two-thirds to a scant 1 cup of liquid, then remove from the heat and stir in salt and pepper to taste. Set aside, covered, until you are ready to assemble the dish.

Pancetta

4 very thin slices pancetta

The oven should still be at 300 degrees F. Trim the pancetta slices into disks about 3 1/2 inches in diameter. Line a baking sheet with parchment paper and place the disks on the paper. Cover with another sheet of parchment and top with another baking sheet of the same size in order to keep the disks lying flat. Bake for 45 to 50 minutes, or until the circles are golden brown and crisp. Drain on paper towels until you are ready to assemble the dish.

Polenta

1 3/4 cups chicken stock (see page 136)
3/4 cup coarse yellow cornmeal or polenta
1/3 cup heavy cream

1/4 cup unsalted butter
Salt and freshly ground white pepper

In a large, heavy saucepan, bring the chicken stock to a simmer over medium-high heat. Sprinkle in the cornmeal in a steady stream, whisking all the time in the same direction until it is completely blended in. Reduce the heat to low, switch to a wooden spoon or paddle, and stir every 2 to 3 minutes for about 35 minutes, or until the polenta grains have softened, adding more chicken stock as necessary if the mixture becomes too thick to stir. During the last 5 minutes of cooking, stir in the cream, butter and salt and pepper to taste. The finished polenta should be creamy and very thick.

Assembly

1 tablespoon extra virgin olive oil
The reserved Santa Barbara shrimp and the reserved shrimp jus
1/3 cup unsalted butter at room temperature, cut into 3 pieces
16 baby asparagus tips, blanched for 4 minutes in boiling water and refreshed in ice water
8 halves sun-dried tomatoes, soaked for 25 minutes in boiling water and squeezed dry
1 teaspoon finely chopped Italian (flat-leaf) parsley

In a large sauté pan, heat the oil over medium-high heat. When very hot, add the shrimp and sauté for 1 to 2 minutes per side, or until just done through and golden. In a medium saucepan over medium heat, bring the jus to a simmer, then pour it into a blender. Blend at high speed, removing the lid to add the butter, a piece at a time, and blending just until emulsified. Return the sauce to the pan and skim off any foam that rises to the surface. Stir in the asparagus, tomatoes and parsley and return to very low heat for 1 minute, stirring, or until just warmed through. Mound some polenta into each of 4 heated serving bowls and place 3 shrimp on each serving. Spoon 4 asparagus tips, 2 sun-dried tomatoes and some sauce over each serving and top it with a disk of pancetta

SOMMELIER'S WINE CHOICE
El Molino Chardonnay (Napa Valley)
Domaine de Comtes Lafon Meursault "Clos de la Barre"
(White Burgundy, Côte de Beaune)

Calves' Brains

WITH SAUTÉED BABY ARTICHOKES AND BALSAMIC VINEGAR

SERVES 4

Calves' brains are available by special order from kosher butchers.
After the soaking and blanching process, the brains could be refrigerated overnight, if desired.

Brains

1 teaspoon red wine vinegar
1 pound calves' brains, soaked in cold, slowly running water to cover for 3 to 4 hours to remove the blood

In a medium saucepan, bring a generous amount of lightly salted water to a boil and add the vinegar. Remove from the heat and add the calves' brains. Allow the brains to rest in the hot cooking water until completely cool, then drain on paper towels and remove the skin and fibers, taking care not to damage each one too much. Cover and refrigerate until ready to finish the dish.

Artichokes

10 baby or 5 large artichokes, trimmed into bottoms and choke removed (see page 139)
2 tablespoons unsalted butter
1 medium shallot, finely chopped

Slice the artichoke bottoms into 1/8-inch-thick slices. In a medium sauté pan, heat the butter over medium heat and sauté the artichokes, stirring frequently, for 4 to 5 minutes, or until tender and golden. Add the shallot and cook for 1 minute more, then remove from the heat. Cover and set aside while you make the sauce.

SOMMELIER'S WINE CHOICE
Dr. Heger Spätburgunder (Pinot Noir, Baden)
Talley Pinot Noir (Arroyo Grande Valley)

Sauce

1 tablespoon unsalted butter
3 medium shallots, finely chopped
2/3 cup balsamic vinegar, over 5 years old, if possible
2 cups red wine
1 cup veal stock (see page 138)

In a medium saucepan, melt the butter over medium heat. Add the shallots and sauté for 3 to 4 minutes, or until softened. Add the vinegar to the pan and deglaze, stirring and scraping the bottom and sides to release all the flavorful bits into the liquid. Reduce the vinegar by half, then add the wine and stock and reduce the mixture by two-thirds, until the liquid is syrupy and only about 1 cup remains. Set aside, covered, until you are ready to finish the dish.

Finishing

2 teaspoons all-purpose flour
Salt and freshly ground black pepper
The reserved calves' brains
2 tablespoons unsalted butter, for cooking the brains
The reserved sauce
1/3 cup unsalted butter, at room temperature, cut into 3 pieces, for finishing the sauce
2 tablespoons finely chopped chives
1/8 teaspoon coarsely cracked black pepper

Sprinkle a little flour and salt and pepper to taste evenly over the brains. In a medium heavy sauté pan, heat the butter over medium-high heat until it is just brown. Add the brains and sauté in the browned butter for 2 to 4 minutes on each side, or until golden. Drain briefly on paper towels.

Bring the reserved sauce back to a simmer over medium-high heat, then reduce the heat to low and swirl in the butter, a piece at a time, stirring and swirling just until emulsified. Remove the sauce from the heat and stir in the chives and pepper.

On each of 4 heated appetizer plates, mound one-quarter of the sliced artichoke bottoms and perch a section of brains on top. Drizzle a little of the sauce onto the plate around the artichokes.

Sardines "A Day in Nice"

SERVES 4

I conceived this dish on a day when my nostalgia for the Mediterranean was strong (thinking of Nice always makes me feel as if I'm on vacation). It is imperative to find perfectly fresh sardines for this dish.

Vegetables

1/4 cup extra virgin olive oil
1 head fennel (about 12 ounces), tough outer layer removed and the flesh cut into thin julienne strips, feathery tops reserved for garnish
4 very ripe plum tomatoes, peeled, seeded and diced (see page 139)
1/3 cup (2 ounces) niçoise olives, pitted and halved
1 tablespoon basil chiffonade, about 8 leaves (see page 139)
1 medium shallot, finely chopped
1/2 teaspoon coarsely cracked white pepper

In a medium sauté pan, heat half the oil over medium heat. Add the fennel and sauté for 5 to 6 minutes, stirring occasionally, or until softened. Set aside, covered, until you are ready to assemble the dish.

In a medium mixing bowl, combine the tomatoes, olives, basil, shallot, the remaining oil and the pepper and toss to mix. Set aside.

Sardines

8 sun-dried tomatoes, softened for 20 minutes in hot water, squeezed dry and halved (if available, use Hollywood roof-dried tomatoes, page 21)
8 very fresh sardines, heads, tails and fins removed, carefully filleted to remove all the bones

Lay the 16 sardine fillets on the work surface, with the larger end facing away from you. Place a sun-dried tomato half close to the smaller (tail) end of the fillet and roll the fillets up tightly, then secure with a toothpick. Bring a saucepan of water to a simmer over medium heat and set a steamer inside. Steam the sardine rolls, covered, for 4 to 5 minutes, or until just firm. Remove from the heat.

Assembly

Four 1/4-inch-thick slices country-style white bread, toasted until golden
The reserved tomato and olive mixture
The reserved fennel tops, torn into tiny sprigs, for garnish
Small handful of pale inner leaves from a heart of celery, for garnish (optional)

Reheat the fennel julienne gently until just heated through. On each of 4 heated appetizer plates, place a crouton and mound 1/4 of the fennel over it. Remove the toothpicks from the sardine rolls and balance 4 rolls on top of the fennel on each plate. Spoon a little of the tomato and olive mixture around the fennel and garnish each plate with 2 or 3 sprigs of fennel and a few celery leaves, if desired.

SOMMELIER'S WINE CHOICE
Joseph Phelps Viognier "Vin de Mistral" (Napa Valley)
Alban Vineyards Viognier (San Luis Obispo)

Chicken Quesadillas

WITH AVOCADO AND CILANTRO SALSA

After living in Los Angeles for 10 years, I came up with my own version of the classic quesadilla. These perfect little rounds can be cut into quarters and passed as hors d'oeuvres, if desired. You could use chicken breasts or drumsticks for this recipe, adjusting the cooking time accordingly.

Salsa

2 teaspoons extra virgin olive oil
1/4 small red onion, cut into 1/4-inch dice
3 plum tomatoes, peeled, seeded and cut into
   1/4-inch dice (see page 139)
1 tablespoon tomato juice
1/2 small jalapeño pepper, seeded and minced
  (about 1 teaspoon)

1 small clove garlic, very finely chopped
Pinch of cayenne pepper
Dash of Tabasco
1 tablespoon finely chopped cilantro
Juice of 1/2 lemon
1/2 avocado, cut into 1/4-inch dice
Salt and freshly ground white pepper, to taste

In a small skillet, heat the oil over medium heat. Add the onion and sauté for 2 to 3 minutes, or until translucent. Remove from the heat and allow to cool for 5 minutes. In a medium mixing bowl, combine the remaining salsa ingredients and toss gently together until evenly mixed. Cover and refrigerate until you are ready to serve.

Quesadillas

1 pasilla or Anaheim chili pepper
1/2 pound chicken thighs
3 large flour tortillas

3/4 cup Monterey Jack cheese, grated
4 plum tomatoes, peeled and thinly sliced
  (see page 139)
2 tablespoons finely chopped cilantro

Preheat a grill or broiler to high heat. Grill the pepper, turning, until evenly charred, then place it in a brown paper bag and seal the bag. When the pepper is cool enough to handle, peel, seed and cut it into 4 equal squares. At the same time, grill the chicken thighs, turning to brown them evenly, for 8 to 12 minutes, or until they are done through with no trace of pink remaining. When they are cool enough to handle, slice the meat thinly and set it aside, discarding the bones.

    Using a 3-inch cookie cutter, cut each tortilla into three 3-inch disks. You should have 9 equal disks (you will only use 8 – the 9th is a chef's perk).

    Assemble four 3-inch open ring molds on a tray that will fit into your refrigerator and place one of the tortilla disks in the bottom of each mold. Divide the quesadilla ingredients among the molds, layering them as follows: a little grated cheese, sliced tomato, chicken, pepper squares, chopped cilantro and a little more cheese. Cover each mold with another tortilla disk and press down gently but firmly to compact the layers. Refrigerate the quesadillas for 2 or 3 hours to help them firm up before you finish the dish.

Finishing

1/4 cup corn oil
Cayenne pepper
The reserved salsa
4 sprigs cilantro

In a large nonstick skillet, heat 1 tablespoon of the oil over medium heat. Remove the ring molds from the layered quesadillas, holding the top down with 2 fingers as you lift the mold up and away. Then, using a flat-ended spatula, transfer the quesadillas 2 at a time to the skillet and sauté until they are just barely golden and the cheese has melted, about 1 minute on each side. Press down gently on the top before turning each one so that the cheese will adhere to the tortilla and the quesadilla will hold together. Add another tablespoon of the oil before cooking the next 2 quesadillas, if necessary. Transfer the cooked quesadillas to 4 heated appetizer plates, sprinkle a little cayenne pepper around the rim of the plate, and serve immediately, topped with a spoonful of salsa and a sprig of cilantro.

SOMMELIER'S WINE CHOICE
Calera Viognier (Central Coast)
Qupé Viognier (Santa Barbara)

Chicken Quesadillas
WITH AVOCADO AND CILANTRO SALSA

SERVES 4

After living in Los Angeles for 10 years, I came up with my own version of the classic quesadilla. These perfect little rounds can be cut into quarters and passed as hors d'oeuvres, if desired. You could use chicken breasts or drumsticks for this recipe, adjusting the cooking time accordingly.

Salsa

2 teaspoons extra virgin olive oil
1/4 small red onion, cut into 1/4-inch dice
3 plum tomatoes, peeled, seeded and cut into
    1/4-inch dice (see page 139)
1 tablespoon tomato juice
1/2 small jalapeño pepper, seeded and minced
    (about 1 teaspoon)

1 small clove garlic, very finely chopped
Pinch of cayenne pepper
Dash of Tabasco
1 tablespoon finely chopped cilantro
Juice of 1/2 lemon
1/2 avocado, cut into 1/4-inch dice
Salt and freshly ground white pepper, to taste

In a small skillet, heat the oil over medium heat. Add the onion and sauté for 2 to 3 minutes, or until translucent. Remove from the heat and allow to cool for 5 minutes. In a medium mixing bowl, combine the remaining salsa ingredients and toss gently together until evenly mixed. Cover and refrigerate until you are ready to serve.

Quesadillas

1 pasilla or Anaheim chili pepper
1/2 pound chicken thighs
3 large flour tortillas

3/4 cup Monterey Jack cheese, grated
4 plum tomatoes, peeled and thinly sliced
    (see page 139)
2 tablespoons finely chopped cilantro

Preheat a grill or broiler to high heat. Grill the pepper, turning, until evenly charred, then place it in a brown paper bag and seal the bag. When the pepper is cool enough to handle, peel, seed and cut it into 4 equal squares. At the same time, grill the chicken thighs, turning to brown them evenly, for 8 to 12 minutes, or until they are done through with no trace of pink remaining. When they are cool enough to handle, slice the meat thinly and set it aside, discarding the bones.

  Using a 3-inch cookie cutter, cut each tortilla into three 3-inch disks. You should have 9 equal disks (you will only use 8 – the 9th is a chef's perk).

  Assemble four 3-inch open ring molds on a tray that will fit into your refrigerator and place one of the tortilla disks in the bottom of each mold. Divide the quesadilla ingredients among the molds, layering them as follows: a little grated cheese, sliced tomato, chicken, pepper squares, chopped cilantro and a little more cheese. Cover each mold with another tortilla disk and press down gently but firmly to compact the layers. Refrigerate the quesadillas for 2 or 3 hours to help them firm up before you finish the dish.

Finishing

1/4 cup corn oil
Cayenne pepper
The reserved salsa
4 sprigs cilantro

In a large nonstick skillet, heat 1 tablespoon of the oil over medium heat. Remove the ring molds from the layered quesadillas, holding the top down with 2 fingers as you lift the mold up and away. Then, using a flat-ended spatula, transfer the quesadillas 2 at a time to the skillet and sauté until they are just barely golden and the cheese has melted, about 1 minute on each side. Press down gently on the top before turning each one so that the cheese will adhere to the tortilla and the quesadilla will hold together. Add another tablespoon of the oil before cooking the next 2 quesadillas, if necessary. Transfer the cooked quesadillas to 4 heated appetizer plates, sprinkle a little cayenne pepper around the rim of the plate, and serve immediately, topped with a spoonful of salsa and a sprig of cilantro.

SOMMELIER'S WINE CHOICE
Calera Viognier (Central Coast)
Qupé Viognier (Santa Barbara)

HOT APPETIZERS

Scallop Roll

WITH BROWN BUTTER VINAIGRETTE AND LONG CHIVES

SERVES 6

This is one of the original dishes that was born with the Patina restaurant. Over the years it has become a favorite of many of our customers.
This is yet another dish that will be much easier if you have a mandoline.

Potatoes

1/4 cup unsalted butter, melted
Salt and freshly ground white pepper
1 large or 2 medium Idaho potatoes, peeled and trimmed flat on one long edge to form a
    beginning surface for slicing

Preheat the oven to 350 degrees F. Line a baking sheet with parchment paper, brush it with some of the butter, then sprinkle with a little salt and pepper. With a mandoline or a sharp knife, cut the potatoes carefully lengthwise into 1/8-inch-thick oval slices and arrange them in a single layer on the baking sheet (you will need 12 slices). Brush the potatoes well with the butter and sprinkle with a little more salt and pepper. Cover with another sheet of parchment paper and bake the potato slices for 10 to 12 minutes, or until just tender. Set aside until cool enough to handle.

Scallop Rolls

1 cup loosely packed spinach leaves, stems removed
12 large sea scallops (about 1 1/2 ounces each)
Salt and freshly ground white pepper
1 medium shallot, finely chopped

Lay an 8-inch-long sheet of plastic wrap on the work surface. By slightly overlapping 3 slices of potato parallel in the center of the plastic, create a 4-inch by 6-inch sheet with rounded edges. Place 3 or 4 spinach leaves on the sheet, arranging them to cover it completely; place 2 scallops at the top of one short end of the sheet. Season to taste with salt and pepper and sprinkle with a little of the shallot. Roll the scallops up tightly in the potato and spinach, using the plastic wrap to help roll, and seal the plastic tightly. Repeat the process to make the other 5 rolls, and refrigerate them for 1 to 2 hours to become firm.

Cooking

1 teaspoon clarified butter (see page 136)

Have all the ingredients for the sauce ready before you cook the scallop rolls. Remove the plastic wrap from the scallop rolls and place them carefully near the stove. Heat a large nonstick skillet over medium heat, add the butter, and when it is very hot, sauté the rolls for about 2 minutes, until they are crisp and golden, turning gently with kitchen tongs to brown all sides evenly. Keep the rolls warm in a low oven while you quickly finish the sauce.

Sauce

1/3 cup unsalted butter, for the first step of the sauce
2 tablespoons balsamic vinegar
1/3 cup unsalted butter at room temperature, cut into 3 pieces, for finishing the sauce
Salt and freshly ground black pepper
3 plum tomatoes, peeled, seeded and diced (see page 139), for garnish
2 medium shallots, finely chopped, for garnish
1 small bunch of chives, cut into 2-inch lengths, for garnish

In a small sauté pan, melt the first 1/3 cup butter over medium-high heat. Watching carefully, swirl the butter until it turns golden brown, then add the vinegar, standing back, as it will splatter. Reduce the heat, swirl in the remaining 3 pieces of butter, stirring and swirling until the sauce is just thickened and emulsified, then immediately remove it from the heat and season to taste with salt and pepper. Transfer a scallop roll to each of 6 heated appetizer plates and spoon a little of the sauce over the top. Garnish the edges of the plate with the diced tomatoes, shallots and chives.

SOMMELIER'S WINE CHOICE
Georg Bruer Riesling "Chartawein" (Rheingau)
Girard Chardonnay "Reserve" (Napa Valley)

Sautéed Duck Liver
WITH CARAMELIZED MANGO AND GINGER

SERVES 4

Many of us are passionate lovers of duck liver or, as it is called in France, foie gras (see page 140 for a listing of mail-order sources). For those with high cholesterol, however, this dish should be a once-a-year indulgence only.

Ginger

(make 3 hours before serving)
2 ounces fresh ginger, peeled and cut into julienne strips (about 1/2 cup)
2 tablespoons granulated sugar
2 cups water

In a medium saucepan, combine the ginger, sugar and water over medium heat and bring to a boil. Reduce the heat and simmer the ginger slowly, stirring occasionally, for 20 to 30 minutes, or until the liquid has become syrupy. Watch carefully at the end to prevent the syrup from caramelizing. Remove the ginger julienne and spread on parchment paper to dry, using 2 forks to separate the threads. Allow to dry for 3 hours. (The ginger will still be sticky and soft, not hard and brittle.)

Caramelized Mango

1 ripe mango, peeled and cut into 4 equal pieces (2 slices from each side); discard the pit
2 tablespoons raw or turbinado sugar

Preheat the broiler to high heat. Slice each of the mango pieces into 1/4-inch slices, leaving them attached at the top so that they resemble a fan, and fan them out on a lightly oiled baking sheet. Sprinkle the sugar evenly over the top. Place under the hot broiler and cook until the sugar has caramelized, watching carefully all the time so that they do not burn. Set aside.

SOMMELIER'S WINE CHOICE
Mumm Sparkling Wine "Cuvée Brut" (Napa Valley)
Billecart Salmon Brut Rosé (Champagne)

Sauce

2 tablespoons granulated sugar
2 teaspoons water
2 tablespoons minced fresh ginger
1 teaspoon lemon juice
1 cup veal stock (see page 138)
2 tablespoons unsalted butter, at room temperature
1/2 teaspoon vodka
Pinch of cayenne pepper

Refer to page 139 for the technique of making caramel, then follow the instructions, combining the sugar and water in a small heavy saucepan. Just before the caramel is dark brown, add the minced ginger. Stir for 30 seconds, then add the lemon juice to the caramel mixture (it may spatter). Slowly add the veal stock, stirring all the time, and return the pan to medium-high heat. Simmer the sauce for about 10 minutes, until it is the consistency of a light syrup and will coat the back of a spoon. Remove the sauce from the heat and swirl in the butter, stirring constantly until it is absorbed. Stir in the vodka and pepper and set the sauce aside at the back of the stove while you finish the dish. Stir it occasionally to prevent a skin from forming.

Assembly

1 tablespoon all-purpose flour
3/4 pound fresh "A" grade duck liver, cut into 4 slices approximately 1/2-inch thick

Preheat the oven to 400 degrees F. Sprinkle a little of the flour on both sides of each duck liver slice and shake off the excess. Heat a dry heavy saute pan over medium-high heat until it is very, very hot. Sauté the slices for 30 seconds on each side, or until browned and crisp, then place them in a small roasting pan and finish cooking in the hot oven for 2 to 3 minutes, or until the liver is soft to the touch.

Place 1 escalope on each of 4 heated appetizer plates and arrange a fan of caramelized mango opposite the liver, with the base of the fan tucked underneath. If desired, add to the sauce a little of the fat from the roasting pan in which you finished cooking the liver. Swirl to mix and spoon some sauce over the liver and mango. Garnish with a small pile of the candied ginger.

Stuffed Zucchini Flowers

WITH TRUFFLES "A LA MAXIMIN"

SERVES 4

I learned this recipe at the side of the great Jacques Maximin of Le Chantecler restaurant in Nice. I am glad to have passed this memorable dish along to the team of people who work with me at Patina, and now to the readers of this book.

Zucchini Flowers

16 baby zucchini with their flowers attached

With a vegetable peeler, carefully peel the end of the zucchini opposite the flower about 1/2 inch in from the end. Reserve the peelings for the zucchini mousse. Have ready a bowl of ice water and bring a medium saucepan of lightly salted water to the boil. Blanch the zucchini with their attached flowers for 5 to 10 seconds, then plunge them gently into the ice water and set them on a tea towel to drain.

Zucchini Mousse

2 slices white bread, crust removed, and torn into bite-sized pieces
2 tablespoons heavy cream
1 tablespoon extra virgin olive oil
2 medium zucchini, skin and outermost 1/2 inch of flesh removed in strips all the way around, center core discarded, blanched for 1 minute in boiling water and drained
5 leaves fresh basil
1 large egg, lightly beaten
Salt and freshly ground white pepper

In a small bowl, combine the bread with the cream, mash together briefly and set aside. In a medium sauté pan, heat the oil over medium-low heat and sauté the zucchini strips along with the baby zucchini trimmings for 2 to 3 minutes, or until al dente. Do not allow to brown. In a food processor fitted with the metal blade, combine the cooked zucchini, basil, egg and bread mixture and process for 1 to 2 minutes, or until completely smooth, scraping down the sides of the bowl as necessary. Season to taste with salt and pepper and place in a pastry bag fitted with a medium-sized plain round tip. If you don't have a pastry bag, place in a small bowl.

SOMMELIER'S WINE CHOICE
Evesham Wood Pinot Noir (Willamette Valley)
Chalone Pinot Noir (Monterey)

Sauce

1/4 cup truffle jus (see page 139)
1/2 cup unsalted butter at room temperature, cut into 4 pieces
2 ounces fresh or canned truffle, thinly sliced
Pinch freshly ground pepper

In a small saucepan, bring the truffle jus to a simmer over medium heat and reduce by about one-quarter. Swirl in the butter a piece at a time, stirring and swirling just until fully emulsified. Stir in the sliced truffle and set aside for 5 minutes to infuse the flavor of the truffle into the sauce. Add the pepper (the truffle jus has enough salt). Set aside.

Finishing and Assembly

2 tablespoons extra virgin olive oil
Salt and freshly ground white pepper
The reserved baby zucchini
The zucchini mousse
2 tablespoons heavy cream, whipped to soft peaks
2 tablespoons whole fresh chervil leaves

Preheat the oven to 325 degrees F. Brush a baking sheet with some of the oil and sprinkle with a little salt and pepper. Gently blow into the flower of each zucchini so that it inflates and you can remove the orange pistils. Pipe or spoon a little of the mousse inside the flower, then twist the end of the flower closed so that it forms a natural knot to seal the mousse inside. (This is more easily accomplished with 2 people!) Arrange the mousse-filled zucchini on the baking sheet, drizzle with a little more of the oil, season again and cover with aluminum foil. Bake in the oven for 10 to 12 minutes, or until the zucchini are heated through but still bright green.

Reheat the sauce gently and whisk in the whipped cream. Slice the main body part of each zucchini lengthwise into several slices, leaving them attached at the flower end, and place 4 zucchini on each of 4 large heated dinner plates, fanning the slices out. Spoon a little of the sauce over and garnish with a few chervil leaves.

Warm Tower of Portobello Mushrooms
FOIE GRAS AND ROASTED SQUAB BREAST WITH ITS VINAIGRETTE

SERVES 4

This recipe was created by Octavio Becerra, who started out with us at Patina and is now the chef/partner at Pinot Bistro, our sister restaurant in the San Fernando Valley.

Squab Confit

(make at least 3 hours before serving or the night before)
4 whole squabs, about 1 pound each
2 cups rendered duck fat

Preheat the oven to 300 degrees F. Set the squabs on a cutting board and remove the legs and thighs. Make a shallow cut down either side of the breastbone and remove the individual breasts without any bones. Rewrap the breasts, hearts and livers together and refrigerate until ready for the final assembly; freeze the carcasses for future stocks or sauces.

Place the legs and thighs in a small braising or roasting pan and completely cover with the duck fat. On the top of the stove, heat the mixture until it is just below a simmer and then bake in the preheated oven for about 2 1/2 hours, or until the meat is falling off the bones. Remove from the oven and allow to cool in the fat. When cool enough to handle, remove the meat from the bones and shred it. Strain, refrigerate and reserve the duck fat for another use, such as sautéing potato. Cover the shredded confit and set aside until you are ready to assemble the dish.

Portobello Mushrooms

2 tablespoons unsalted butter
2 cloves garlic, finely chopped
2 medium shallots, finely chopped
4 large portobello mushroom caps
1 1/2 cups chicken stock (see page 136)
Salt and freshly ground white pepper

Increase the oven temperature to 400 degrees F. In a large ovenproof sauté pan with high sides and a tight-fitting lid or an oval Dutch oven, melt the butter over medium-high heat and add the garlic and shallots. Stir over the heat for 1 minute, then add the mushrooms, top side down, and sauté for 2 to 3 minutes, or until brown. Turn and cook for a further 3 minutes on the other side. Add the stock and salt and pepper to taste and cover.

Braise in the already hot oven for 10 to 15 minutes, or until the mushrooms are just barely tender, turning them over halfway through the cooking time. Remove from the oven, uncover and set the mushrooms aside to cool in the braising liquid.

Walnut Vinaigrette

3 tablespoons champagne vinegar
Salt and freshly ground white pepper
1/2 cup plus 1 tablespoon walnut oil

In a small bowl, whisk the vinegar with salt and pepper to taste. Add the oil in a thin stream, whisking all the time, until the mixture is emulsified. If the mixture is too thick, add a little water to thin it down, 1 teaspoonful at a time. Set aside.

Squab Parts and Jus

2 tablespoons unsalted butter
The reserved squab hearts, livers and breasts
2 sprigs fresh thyme
2 cloves unpeeled garlic, slightly crushed with a chef's knife
Salt and freshly ground white pepper

In a large ovenproof sauté pan, heat 1 tablespoon of the butter over medium heat. Add the hearts and livers and sauté, turning with kitchen tongs, for 2 to 3 minutes, until browned outside but still pink inside. Set aside on an ovenproof plate covered with aluminum foil and wipe out the pan with paper towels.

In the same pan, heat the remaining tablespoon of butter, and when the foam has subsided and the butter is very hot, add the squab breasts, skin side down. Cook the breasts for 2 minutes, then turn over and cook for 1 minute more. Reduce the heat to low and add the thyme, garlic and salt and pepper to the pan. Cook the breasts for 1 to 2 minutes more, basting them with butter from the pan once or twice during the cooking time. The breasts should be pink inside but firm. Set them aside with the hearts and livers and discard the fat from the pan.

Remove the mushrooms from their liquid, drain them and set aside. Add the braising liquid from the mushrooms to the squab-cooking pan and bring to a simmer over medium-high heat. Deglaze the pan, scraping the bottom and sides to release all the flavorful bits into the liquid, and allow it to reduce by about two-thirds, until a scant 1/2 cup of liquid remains. Strain into a bowl through a sieve lined with a double thickness of slightly dampened cheesecloth, pressing down hard on the solids to extract all their flavor. Set the jus aside; discard the solids. *(continued on next page)*

54

Salad

The reserved squab hearts and livers
The reserved squab confit
2 medium shallots, finely chopped
2 tablespoons finely chopped chives
2 tablespoons coarsely chopped walnuts, toasted for 6 minutes in a 350 degree F oven
2 tablespoons of the reserved mushroom braising jus
The reserved walnut vinaigrette
3 cups mizuna greens, arugula, radicchio or other salad greens

Just before you are ready to serve, coarsely chop the hearts and livers, which should still be warm, and combine them in a medium mixing bowl with the squab confit, shallots, chives, toasted walnuts and the braising jus. Toss to mix. Whisk the walnut vinaigrette again just to re-emulsify if it has separated and add the mizuna or salad greens and enough of the vinaigrette to coat all the ingredients to the mixing bowl. Toss until evenly mixed. Reserve some vinaigrette for the assembly.

Assembly

The reserved mushroom caps
8 roasted shallots (see page 138), thinly sliced lengthwise
The reserved squab breasts
Four 2-ounce slices of "A" grade duck liver

Preheat the oven to 400 degrees F. In a large roasting pan, place the mushrooms, caps upward, and fan 2 of the roasted shallots over each one. Place the reserved squab breasts next to them in the pan to reheat. Put the pan in the preheated oven for 2 to 3 minutes, or until warmed through. Meanwhile, heat a dry nonstick pan over very high heat until it is very, very hot and sear the duck liver for 20 seconds on each side. Place 1 slice of duck liver on top of each mushroom, over the roasted shallots, in the oven. Leave the mushrooms in the oven for 1 additional minute to finish cooking the liver, then remove each mushroom, with its topping, to a heated large dinner plate. Pile some of the salad mixture on top of the duck liver, mounding it as high as possible. Slice the squab breasts into three 1-inch slices, fanning one breast out on the very top of each salad. Drizzle a few drops of the remaining walnut vinaigrette around the rims of the plates.

SOMMELIER'S WINE CHOICE
Comte de Vogüé Chambolle Musigny (Red Burgundy, Côtes de Nuits)
Rex Hill Vineyard Pinot Noir (Willamette Valley)

55

Sweetbreads Club Sandwich

WITH APPLE-SMOKED BACON SAUCE

SERVES 4

Buy brioches from your baker and trim them, or substitute a rich butter-topped white bread. The metal rings we use at the restaurant for assembling these towering sandwiches — 3 1/2-inch diameter and 4 inches tall — may be difficult to find; you can improvise your own out of single-serving soup cans with the tops and bottoms removed. Note: If you decide to use chicken liver instead of duck liver for this dish, freezing it for 15 minutes will make it easier to slice.

Sweetbreads

2 tablespoons unsalted butter
1 small carrot, coarsely chopped
1 medium leek, white part only, well rinsed and coarsely chopped
1/4 small onion, coarsely chopped
1 rib celery, coarsely chopped
1 sprig fresh thyme
1 clove garlic, unpeeled
10 ounces veal sweetbreads, soaked in cold, very slowly running water to cover for 4 to 5 hours to rid them of blood

In a medium saucepan, heat the butter over medium-low heat. Add the carrot, leek, onion, celery, thyme and garlic and sweat for 4 to 5 minutes, or until the vegetables are softened but not browned. Add the sweetbreads and enough water to cover them by 1 inch, bring to a simmer and immediately remove from the heat. Allow the sweetbreads to cool in the liquid, then use a sharp knife to trim away the membranes and fibers, taking care not to damage the shape. Set aside, covered, until you are ready to assemble the dish.

Sauce

3/4 cup reduced veal stock (see page 138)
1 slice apple-smoked bacon or other smoky bacon, finely diced and cooked until the fat is rendered, then drained on a paper towel
2 tablespoons unsalted butter at room temperature
1 teaspoon very finely chopped Italian (flat-leaf) parsley
Salt and freshly ground white pepper

In a small saucepan, bring the stock to a simmer over medium-high heat. Add the diced bacon and then the butter, swirling until it is just emulsified. Remove from the heat and add the parsley and salt and pepper to taste. Set aside, covered, until you are ready to assemble the dish.

SOMMELIER'S WINE CHOICE
Bonny Doon Pinot Meunier (Napa Valley)
Gary Farrell Pinot Noir (Russian River)

Preparation

2 tablespoons plus 1/4 cup unsalted butter
2 medium shallots, finely chopped
5 cups spinach leaves, stems removed
Scant 1/2 cup all-purpose flour
Salt and freshly ground white pepper

In a medium sauté pan, heat the 2 tablespoons of butter over medium heat. Add the shallots and cook for 2 to 3 minutes, or until softened. Add the spinach and cook, tossing occasionally, just until wilted. Set aside.

On a plate, combine the flour with salt and pepper to taste and dredge the sweetbreads in the seasoned flour, shaking off the excess. In a large sauté pan, heat the 1/4 cup butter over medium heat. When the foam has subsided and the butter is very hot but not brown, add the sweetbreads and cook for 3 to 4 minutes on each side, or until golden. Drain briefly on paper towels and slice into 8 equal slices.

Assembly

Twelve 3 1/2-inch circles of 1/8-inch-thick brioche or rich white bread, toasted to a golden brown
3 ounces "A" grade duck liver or chicken liver, sliced paper-thin

Preheat the oven to 400 degrees F if you plan to finish the dish right away. Line a baking sheet with parchment paper and place four 3 1/2-inch by 4 inch ring molds on the paper. Place a round of toasted brioche in the bottom of each ring, then add a few leaves of spinach. Follow with a slice of sweetbreads and a few slices of duck liver. Repeat with another layer of brioche, spinach, sweetbreads and liver, then top with a final round of brioche, pressing down firmly to compact the sandwiches. If desired, refrigerate them for 1 to 2 hours.

If the oven is not already on, heat it to 400 degrees F. Gently reheat the sauce, stirring, but do not allow it to boil. Cook the sandwiches in the hot oven for about 2 minutes, or until heated all the way through. Using a flat-ended spatula to slip under the rings, carefully lift each sandwich, in its ring, to the center of a heated serving plate. Gently lift off each ring, holding the sandwich down with 2 fingers, and spoon a little of the warm sauce over the top.

Wienerschnitzel of Artichoke

WITH ROASTED RABBIT LOIN AND CHIVE VINAIGRETTE

SERVES 4

Often I like to play around with the classic dishes, and this is another twist on a classic. I originally created this artichoke "wienerschnitzel" for a vegetarian menu, but added the rabbit later on. You could still make this dish, minus the rabbit, of course, as part of a meat-free menu.

Chive Vinaigrette

2 tablespoons balsamic vinegar
Salt and freshly ground white pepper
1/2 cup plus 1 tablespoon extra virgin olive oil
1 medium shallot, finely chopped
2 tablespoons finely chopped chives

In a small bowl, whisk the balsamic vinegar with salt and pepper to taste. Add the oil in a thin stream, whisking all the time, until the mixture is emulsified. If the vinaigrette is too thick, add a little water to thin it down, 1 teaspoonful at a time. Add the shallot and chives, stir to mix and set aside.

Artichoke "Wienerschnitzels"

Juice of 1 lemon
8 large artichokes, trimmed into bottoms (see page 139)
3 tablespoons extra virgin olive oil

In a large steel saucepan, bring a generous amount of lightly salted water to a boil. Add the lemon juice and artichoke bottoms and cook for about 25 minutes, until the artichokes are tender but still have a little "bite." Drain and cool. Slice 4 of the artichoke bottoms crosswise into four 1/4-inch slices.

On a lightly oiled baking sheet, make the first "wienerschnitzel" by overlapping 4 of the artichoke slices in an oval, trying to create as flat a surface as possible. Repeat with the remaining slices until you have 4 separate ovals.

In a food processor fitted with the metal blade or in a blender, process the remaining 4 artichoke bottoms until very smooth, slowly adding the oil in a thin stream. Spread some of this mousse evenly over each of the 4 artichoke ovals, filling in the holes, and flatten the tops with a spatula. Set the wienerschnitzels aside on the baking sheet, covered with plastic wrap, until you are ready to assemble the dish.

Rabbit

4 rabbit loins
Salt and freshly ground white pepper
2 tablespoons unsalted butter

Preheat a broiler to high heat to be ready for cooking the wienerschnitzels. Season the rabbit loins with salt and pepper to taste. In a large sauté pan, melt the butter over medium-high heat. Sauté the rabbit loins for about 4 to 6 minutes, using kitchen tongs to turn and brown evenly on all sides, until they are golden on the outside and medium-rare inside. Cover and keep warm while you finish the dish.

Assembly

1/4 cup fresh white bread crumbs, ground very fine
The reserved artichoke wienerschnitzels
The reserved vinaigrette

Sprinkle the breadcrumbs evenly over each of the 4 artichoke wienerschnitzels. Place the pan under the hot broiler and grill until the bread crumbs are golden brown, watching carefully so that they do not burn. Using a flat-ended spatula, carefully transfer 1 of the wienerschnitzels to each of 4 heated appetizer plates. Slice the rabbit loins into 1/4-inch-thick slices and fan out a quarter of the slices in a semicircle opposite each wienerschnitzel. Spoon a couple of tablespoons of the vinaigrette over the rabbit and serve immediately.

SOMMELIER'S WINE CHOICE
Prince de Mérode Corton (Red Burgundy, Côte de Beaune)
Cornu Ladoix (Red Burgundy, Côte de Beaune)

LUNCH

12 p.m.

The restaurant opens at 11:30, but it takes until noon for orders to come into the kitchen. Until then the chefs take the time to refill the sugar and spices bins and top up the container of baby vegetables for garnish.

Annie, one of the waitresses, comes in to ask a chef what's in a special dish so that she can describe it to a customer. He explains: "Swiss chard greens down, *shrimp* over, then mustard sauce, celery around the rim." She nods.

Out front customers are entering through an inconspicuous metallic door that's flanked by pampas grass. The first person they see is Joachim's wife, Christine Splichal, who oversees the front of the house and a lot more. She's the daughter of a French pastry-maker, but the diners may never guess it. Christine came to this country to study business administration and has no accent to speak of.

A hostess leads diners to seats in the main dining room, a spare, tasteful space decorated only with minimalist floral displays. The wry, even eccentric, menu systematically plays off the European serious-mindedness of the room. It's lunchtime; people order quickly — salads and pastas and *fish*. The waiters combine a dignified, attentive manner with lunch-break dispatch.

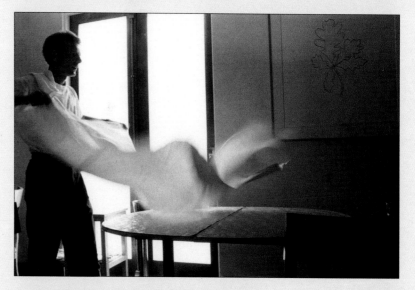

In the kitchen the printer at the pickup station starts clicking out orders. A waiter tears off four of them and gives copies to **Alec**, who calls them out. The chefs all shout "Yes" in reply. Some of the pans they throw meat into are grotesquely warped, as if a strongman has tried to bend them shut. It's because they're kept on burners all day long so that nobody has to wait for a pan to heat up.

There's no "vegetable of the day" at Patina. Each entrée has its own unique garnish, which adds considerably to the work of the kitchen. There are no hot-lamps either. A chef can't finish an order at his own pace and let it sit under a lamp while the rest of the orders for the same table are being finished; every item in a course has to be finished at **exactly the same time.**

Lunch dishes are less elaborate than dinner dishes, but diners are even more insistent on quick service at lunch. In a few minutes Alec and even line chefs start calling out to know when some order is expected to be done. The answers are precise: one minute, 30 seconds, 45 seconds.

"Fire 1 on first course, please."

"How long till you want it?"

"A minute and a half."

"Three minutes on the spa fish."

"Two minutes."

"I need three pieces, one asparagus lamb."

"Tomato ravioli up with main course."

The kitchen is getting hot. "Table 5 has to come out," says Joachim, entering the kitchen. "And 6 and 8," says a chef.

"Al, are you here?" Joachim calls. "Give me a *quesadilla*. Let's go. Is it up or what?" 12:20 p.m. Jonny comes back from a catering gig as Joachim is calling an order: "Fourteen is rush. They want to catch the game on TV." He confers with Jonny. "Are you ready? **Are we gonna run out of oysters?"**

12:35 p.m.

Appetizer plates begin coming back, and the dishwashers start work. Near them a chef methodically slices salmon fillets.

Alec calls: "Fire a spa fish on 12, have both in two minutes."

"OK, two fired."

"And tuna medium-rare. Everybody up in two and a half."

"Roll fire" — meaning, cook a quenelle to be served on a roll.

"Ordering a chicken salad main" — that's a *salad* as a main course. "Pick up first course on 5, baby appetizer" — time for a waiter to pick up the appetizer made with baby vegetables.

"How long on the tuna?" **Joachim** needs to know. "The guy only eats one course."

Alec plates up today's pasta, the *bucatini*, simultaneously pouring and swirling it with tongs to keep the strands neat in the plate. Meanwhile, another chef steps in behind him to keep his onions from burning while he's occupied.

A customer who comes for lunch at least once a week drops by the kitchen to say hello to Joachim. Wants to know when he's leaving town to celebrate his 40th birthday. **"Don't you worry about it,"** Joachim says, joshing. "They know you, they'll take good care of you when I'm not here. You'll get *better* service."

Alec calls out: "Table 4, two pastas and a spa fish, JBS."

"One *whitefish*, sauce on the side."

"Lamb chop, mashed."

"Spa fish now, yes?"

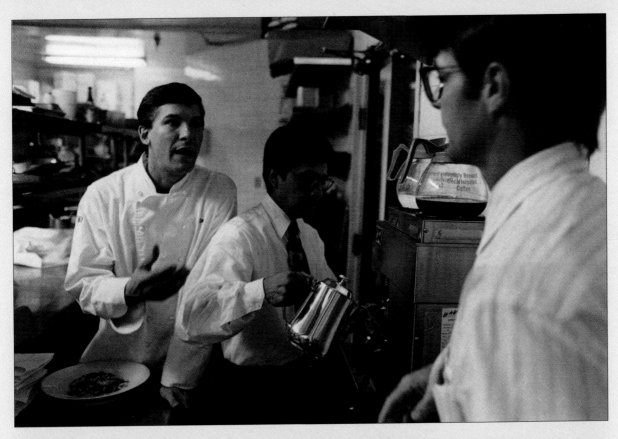

“

He tells us, 'Don't worry about
somebody else stealing
your ideas. Show them all
your cards, but always be working
on a new dish.'

”

Jonny Fernow, Patina executive chef

“

Look at that menu.
He's tapped into
American pop culture,
into Southern California.
People are amazed
at the way this European
guy has his finger
on the pulse of things.

”

*Octavio Becerra, chef/partner
at Pinot Bistro,
former Patina chef de cuisine*

LUNCH

Ready orders are set on a cloth that's taped to the stainless-steel counter; it's there so

that plates don't slip. At the moment, **Joachim** is drawing a diagram on the cloth: a white-

fish roll tied with green onion strings, polenta under, chanterelles all around. "We're gonna

serve it skin side up," he says to Alec. "It makes a nice little package."

He glances at the salmon Alec is arranging as a salad, prods it, shakes his head.

"The *salmon* has to be cooked through," he says. "When people think of salad they think

of fish cooked through." Alec removes the fish from the bed of *asparagus* and

fires it again.

The *portobello mushroom* special is a huge mushroom cap with a ragout of

Maine lobsters on top. Alec puts the onion threads on top of it himself.

"Whitefish with sauce on the side, where is it?"

"Right here, in my hand."

"Three, four and five on table 7."

"Table 5, two spa fish and a salmon salad. Well-done on that salmon."

"Fire 11, one *chicken*, one spa fish."

A Potato Soup

LIKE THE OLD DAYS WITH FLAKY POTATO KNISH

SERVES 4

This is how I remember the comforting potato soup my father used to make when I was a child. The knish sneaked its way into the recipe when I came to live in Los Angeles.

Soup

1/4 cup unsalted butter
1 small onion, coarsely chopped
1 medium leek, white part only, coarsely chopped
1 rib celery, coarsely chopped
1 sprig fresh thyme
4 cloves garlic, crushed with a chef's knife
1 slice apple-smoked bacon or other smoky bacon
1 bay leaf
3 Idaho potatoes, peeled and sliced 1/4 inch thick
1 1/2 cups chicken stock (see page 136)
1 1/2 cups heavy cream
3 tablespoons crème fraîche
Salt and freshly ground white pepper

In a large saucepan, melt the butter over medium heat and add the onion, leek, celery, thyme, garlic, bacon and bay leaf. Sweat the mixture over medium-low heat without allowing it to color at all, stirring occasionally, for 5 to 6 minutes, or until very tender. Add the potatoes, stock and cream. (The liquid should cover the potatoes; if it does not, add a little water.) Bring the mixture to a simmer and cook, partially covered, for about 20 minutes, until the potatoes are tender. Purée the mixture in a blender and add the crème fraîche. Push the soup through a fine strainer into a clean saucepan and season to taste with salt and white pepper. Cover and set aside.

Potatoes are a comforting ingredient. That's one reason why I use them so much. My previous restaurant was a critical success, but it didn't last long. At Patina I didn't want people to feel intimidated.

Knish

1 large Idaho potato, peeled and quartered
1 cup milk
1 cup water
3 tablespoons unsalted butter
2 tablespoons finely chopped yellow onion
1 tablespoon finely chopped Italian (flat-leaf) parsley
Salt and freshly ground white pepper
2 1/4 pounds frozen, prerolled puff pastry, thawed according to package directions and cut into four 3-inch circles and four 4-inch circles
1 large egg, lightly beaten

Preheat the oven to 400 degrees F. In a medium saucepan, combine the potato with the milk and water and bring the mixture to a simmer over medium-high heat. Simmer, partially covered, for about 20 minutes or until the potato is tender.

Meanwhile, in a small sauté pan, heat 1 tablespoon of the butter over medium heat and add the onion. Sauté for 3 to 4 minutes, or until softened, then remove from the heat and stir in the parsley. Put the potato through a food mill or mash with a masher or hand blender and stir in the butter and the parsley mixture. Season to taste with salt and pepper.

Rinse 1 large or 2 small baking sheets with cold water. Set the 4 smaller circles of puff pastry on the sheet(s) and mound about 2 tablespoons of the mashed potato in the center of each circle, leaving the edges clear for attaching the tops. Brush the edges of the circles with a little of the beaten egg. Score each of the 4 larger circles with the back of a knife in a lattice pattern, and using a 1/4-inch aspic or biscuit cutter, cut a small circular vent hole in the center. Form the circles into domes with your hands and fit them over the mounded potatoes, pressing down firmly around the egg-washed edges to form a good seal. Brush the knishes with the remaining egg wash and bake for 10 to 12 minutes, or until puffed and golden.

Assembly

Place a knish in each of 4 heated soup bowls. Reheat the soup gently, if necessary, and serve it in a heated tureen. Ladle some hot soup into each bowl around the knish. Or if you prefer, you can serve the knish on the side.

Cold Spring Pea Soup
WITH YOGURT AND CRUSHED WHITE PEPPER AND MINT

SERVES 6

When I think of warm weather I think of fresh peas and this soup – bright emerald green, fresh and delicious.
Draining the yogurt in the refrigerator overnight makes it thick enough to form "quenelles."

Soup

1/4 cup unsalted butter
1/2 small yellow onion, coarsely chopped
1 small leek, white part only, coarsely chopped
2 ribs celery, coarsely chopped
3 cloves garlic, crushed with a chef's knife
1 sprig fresh thyme
1 slice apple-smoked bacon or other smoky bacon, thickly sliced
3/4 cup dried green split peas, soaked overnight in water to cover
1 quart chicken stock (see page 136)
3 cups (about 1 pound) frozen green peas
Salt and freshly ground white pepper

In a large saucepan, melt the butter over medium heat. Add the onion, leek, celery, garlic, thyme and bacon and cook for 3 to 4 minutes, stirring occasionally, until the vegetables are softened. Add the dried peas and stock and bring the liquid just to a simmer. Cook over low heat, partially covered, for 45 to 50 minutes, or until the peas are perfectly tender. Remove from the heat and allow to cool for 15 minutes, uncovered.

Add the frozen peas to the mixture and stir together (this will immediately chill the soup). Immediately purée the mixture, in batches if necessary, in a food processor fitted with the metal blade or a blender. Process for 3 to 4 minutes, scraping down the sides of the bowl as necessary, until the purée is very smooth. For a perfectly smooth soup, push the purée through a fine strainer. Season to taste with salt and pepper.

Assembly

3/4 cup plain yogurt, drained overnight in a sieve lined with a double thickness of cheesecloth set
  over a bowl in the refrigerator
1/2 teaspoon coarsely cracked white pepper
18 fresh sprigs mint, tops only

Put 6 soup bowls in the refrigerator to chill. Using 2 teaspoons, mold 3 small quenelles of yogurt and place them in the bottom of each chilled bowl. Repeat the process for the remaining 5 bowls. Sprinkle a little white pepper over the top and place a mint sprig in between each quenelle. Serve the soup in a chilled soup tureen and ladle some of the soup into each bowl at the table.

3:00 p.m.

The lunch crew is gone and the dinner crew has drifted in. Part of the dinner prep was done in the morning, but dinner is a more demanding meal than lunch. The afternoon is a steady shift of baking and chopping, searing and poaching.

5:00 p.m. The dinner crew have their own dinner – not the refined dishes they cook every day but rough, undemanding, almost peasanty stuff: Italian bread, hot sausage, baked *spare ribs* with a sauce thrown together from tomatoes, basil, red pepper and half-raw chopped garlic.

5:30 p.m. As the first few guests arrive, the chefs are in the kitchen finishing last-minute prep: chopping spinach, frying *artichoke chips*, cutting perfectly even slices of *leek greens* (taken from a plastic tub labeled "pecans" – it was probably once used for that purpose), laying out potato "bricks" – shoebox-sized tangles of potato cut wire-thin and deep-fried – and other fried garnishes, such as carrot threads, beet chips, steamed green onions and baby bok choy cabbages. One waiter is folding napkins on the counter while another polishes plates with a napkin; a third slices loaf after loaf of bread. A line chef wanders around asking where in hell she can find a ladle. Another chef calls out: "Jonny, the oven's breaking down every 10 minutes. What'd they do to it yesterday?"

Joachim walks in talking to a waiter: "Just let us know which one is the birthday guy.

I hear they've been discussing this party since October, and she's obviously very picky." He confers with Jonny about the oven. Another problem: the light over the restaurant entrance has been flickering on and off. A list of 24-hour repair companies is posted next to the telephone.

5:45 p.m. Christine Splichal sticks her head in the door, smiles at everybody and exchanges a few quiet words with Joachim. The first order comes in. **Stephen**, the sous-chef, calls out jovially, **"Everybody ready to go? Fire the veal."** He salts and peppers a *veal loin* and throws it in a pan.

Joachim comes back into the kitchen and reports that a party of 60 people has canceled. For many restaurants this would be a disaster, but Patina has a waiting list, so the cancellation means only that the private dining rooms will fill up later than expected. "We'll have two parties from the Beverly Hills Hotel around ten," he says, "each with bodyguards. I assume they're Arabs." Tubs of vegetables for garnish are coming down from the prep kitchen upstairs, where three more chefs are working.

"Pick up shrimp on 5."

Joachim pops in again to remind one of the chefs to watch over the work of a new employee.

"Taste everything he cooks. He sends out nothing on his own."

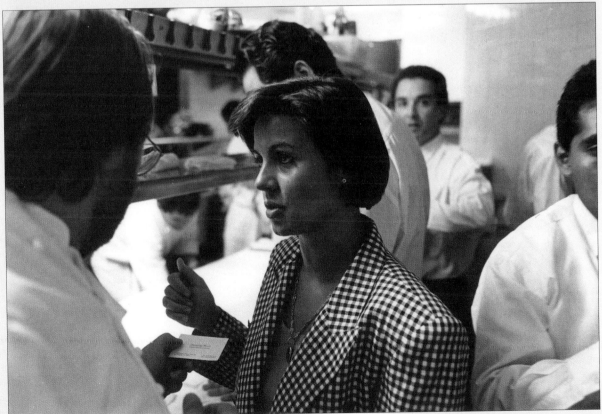

Christine is a big part of his
success, with her administrative
skills and her background
in the food business. They're
a perfect match.
"

Octavio Becerra, chef/partner
at Pinot Bistro,
former Patina chef de cuisine

“

It's not like making a movie, where you have a final product.
Each day is another show – two shows, a lunch show and a dinner show –

Line Cook

Pastry Cook

Dishwasher

and you're only as good as your last performance.
"

Prep Cooks

Line Cook

Prep Cook

EARLY SATURDAY NIGHT, KITCHEN

6:30 p.m.

Jonny reads an order slip. "Two truffle risottos," he calls. "You hear me, homies?" When the risotto is dished up, Joachim takes over. He no longer cooks on the line, but he still tastes everything before it goes out. He also usually shaves the truffle for this dish, which is available only in season and doesn't appear on the menu.

Another item not on the regular menu is *veal loin*. Saturday brings out the meat eaters, and on Saturday Patina always serves veal loin in mustard cream sauce, balanced on a Brillo pad-like nest of fried potatoes on top of a bed of mashed potatoes.

6:45 p.m. Orders are coming into a small kitchen printer from the waiters' computer stations out front. The 5:30 crowd, early eaters on their way to the theater, are mostly gone now, and the dining room is filling up again. Back waiter Laurent comes in and confers quietly with Joachim in French.

"Ordering blinis."

"Who's heating up the duck confit?" Joachim calls. "Let's go, we've got 20 people."

Another waiter asks Joachim if one of his diners can make a substitution in the prix-fixe menu; OK. "And **fire me a shrimp** menu right now," Joachim calls to the line. "The new table is trying to get to the theater. And Lily Tomlin just came in" — meaning that the comedienne has just made a reservation for later in the evening. He settles into his customary post between the coffee machine and the door to oversee the kitchen, which is getting busier by the moment.

He imparts his standards to everyone who works for him. I remember him standing in front of us saying, 'Did you taste that? Don't put it on a plate if you haven't tasted it.' He's on top of every plate that comes out of his kitchen, and there aren't a lot of chefs like that.

Traci Des Jardins, chef at Rubicon, San Francisco,
former Patina chef de cuisine

7:00 p.m. The kitchen is in a collective fury. Waiters are sticking their heads in the door to ask the chefs for exact estimates of how long it's going to take for their courses to be ready. "There was not enough salt and pepper on the confit," **Joachim thunders**. "And I don't want to see any liver seared on one side only." He studies the order slips and points to two chefs. "You prep and he does the serving. Otherwise we're gonna go down."

Laurent reappears. "Laurent," says Joachim. "Is the party cleared? Check it." He turns back to the line chefs. "Where's the onion salad?"

He takes over the saucing of a *shrimp appetizer* and discovers that the shrimp are smaller than usual. "I was telling you this morning," Jonny says to him. "Because of the weather in Santa Barbara, this is all we can get."

Joachim tells the chef who was working on the appetizer to use three shrimp when they're so small. He starts getting worked up and growls, "We've always got to have the biggest shrimps! This is gonna cost us a lot of money!"

Whole Roasted Rockfish
BARDED WITH BAY LEAVES AND SWEET GARLIC

SERVES 4

Sometimes I think we cooks have been spoiled by the ease of cooking everything on the grill. Even in a restaurant as elegant as Patina, I like to keep some things on the menu "family-style," served on a platter. Rockfish is a term applied to several different fish, most commonly Pacific or Atlantic Ocean perch, redfish and Pacific red snapper. All are suitable for this dish.

Rockfish

6 cloves garlic peeled
1 whole rockfish (about 3 1/2 to 4 pounds), scaled and gutted
6 fresh bay leaves, snipped in half lengthwise with scissors

Bring a small saucepan of water to a boil and blanch the garlic cloves for 1 minute. Drain, refill the pan with cold water and bring to a boil. Blanch the garlic for 1 minute more, then drain again. Repeat the process a third time, then slice the garlic cloves into slivers.

Put the fish on a work surface and use a small sharp knife to make shallow incisions under the skin all over the fish, without cutting into the flesh. Alternately, insert garlic slivers and halved bay leaves into the incisions, leaving half the length sticking out like scales. Cover the fish with aluminum foil and set aside while you prepare the vegetables.

Vegetables

1/2 cup extra virgin olive oil
1 medium yellow onion, cut into 1/4-inch julienne strips
2 hearts of celery (about 10 ounces), each one cut into quarters, pale inner leaves reserved for garnish
1 head fennel (about 1/2 pound), tough outer layer removed and cut into 4 equal wedges, feathery tops reserved for garnish
1/2 teaspoon coarsely cracked black peppercorns
8 small Yukon Gold or other yellow potatoes, each one peeled and cut into 8 wedges
1/2 cup dry white wine
1 1/2 cups chicken stock (see page 136)

Preheat the oven to 400 degrees F. In a large oval braising pan or Dutch oven large enough to hold the whole fish, heat half of the oil over medium heat. Add the onion and sauté for 3 to 4 minutes, or until just softened. Add the celery, fennel, peppercorns and potatoes and continue to sauté, stirring occasionally, for 5 to 6 minutes, or until all the vegetables are slightly softened but not browned. Add the wine, remaining oil and stock, cover the pan and simmer for 7 to 8 minutes, or until the vegetables are al dente.

Finishing and Assembly

The reserved fish
The reserved fennel tops
The reserved celery leaves
1 teaspoon sea salt

Place the fish, right side up, in the pan on top of the vegetables and baste with the pan juices. Put the pan in the hot oven and roast, basting occasionally, for 25 to 30 minutes, or until the fish is just done to medium.

Place the fish on a large, heated oval platter and surround with all the vegetables jumbled together. Garnish with a few feathery fennel tops and celery leaves and sprinkle with sea salt. Serve the platter at the table.

SOMMELIER'S WINE CHOICE:
Au Bon Climat Chardonnay "Bien Nacido" (Santa Barbara)
Grgich Hills Chardonnay (Napa Valley)

"
There's so much going on inside that head of his. He speaks five or six languages, and sometimes in the heat of battle he can't come out with a single word. So he says, 'Give me the . . . thing, the thing!' After a while you know right away what the thing is.
"

Octavio Becerra, chef/partner at Pinot Bistro,
former Patina chef de cuisine

Maine Lobster "Return from Thailand"

SERVES 4

The diverse ethnic influences here in Los Angeles gave birth to this dish. Lemon grass is one of a number of Thai ingredients that have become popular and are easy to find almost everywhere. It has a pungent, fresh-tasting flavor, but be sure to remove the tough outer layer of skin from the stalk before slicing it. Note: If fresh lemon grass is unavailable, substitute 1 teaspoon of finely chopped lemon zest and 1 tablespoon of lemon juice.

Lobsters #1

4 Maine lobsters, about 1 1/2 pounds each and very much alive

In a very large saucepan, bring a generous amount of water to a boil, and in batches if necessary, plunge the lobsters into boiling water, cover the pan and blanch for 1 minute, then remove them and drain. (The lobsters will be instantly killed.) When cool enough to handle, cut each into 7 pieces as follows: 2 claws, 2 arms, 1 tail, and the head, halved lengthwise. Place all the parts except the heads in a large bowl, cover with a tea towel and refrigerate. Immediately go on to make the stock.

Curried Lobster Stock

The reserved lobster heads
1/4 cup extra virgin olive oil
1 to 2 tablespoons mild curry powder, or to taste
  (from a Thai market if possible)
1 cup white wine
2 medium shallots, coarsely chopped

1 small carrot, coarsely chopped
2 tablespoons peeled and sliced fresh ginger
4 cloves garlic, unpeeled
1 sprig fresh thyme
1 tablespoon cognac
1 quart lobster stock (see page 137)

Preheat the oven to 400 degrees F. Place the lobster heads in a large roasting pan and drizzle with half of the oil. Sprinkle with the curry powder and roast for 15 to 20 minutes, or until bright red and beginning to caramelize. Remove from the oven and add the wine to the pan. Deglaze the pan, stirring and scraping the bottom and sides to release all the flavorful bits into the liquid. Set aside.

In a large, heavy saucepan, heat the remaining oil over medium heat. Add the shallots, carrot and ginger and sauté, stirring occasionally, for 3 to 4 minutes, or until softened. Add the lobster heads with their deglazing liquid, the garlic, thyme and cognac and cook, stirring, for 5 minutes. Add the stock and bring the liquid to a boil. Reduce the heat and simmer for 1 hour, skimming off fats and impurities as necessary. Strain the stock through a strainer lined with a double thickness of slightly dampened cheesecloth into a small saucepan, pressing down hard on the solids to extract all their flavor. Discard the solids.

Over medium-high heat, reduce the stock until there are about 2 cups of liquid remaining. Set aside, covered, until you are ready for the final assembly.

Lobsters #2

The reserved lobster parts
2 tablespoons extra virgin olive oil
4 scallions, white and light green part only, thinly sliced on the diagonal
1 medium leek, white part only, cut into fine julienne strips
4 medium shallots, cut into fine julienne strips
1 tablespoon finely sliced lemon grass
1/3 teaspoon Thai red curry paste
The reserved curried lobster stock
1/2 cup unsalted butter at room temperature, cut into 4 pieces
Salt and freshly ground white pepper
1 tablespoon mint chiffonade (see page 139), about 8 leaves

Crack the shells of the reserved claws and arms, but do not remove the meat (this will make it easier for your guests to do so later). Cut the tails in half lengthwise, leaving the meat in the shells. In a large sauté pan with high sides, heat the oil over medium-high heat. Add the tails, cut side down, and sauté for 3 to 4 minutes, or until they are browned but still rare (they will be cooked again later). Set the tails aside and add the claws and arms to the same pan. Sauté until the shells turn a bright red, about 4 minutes. Add the scallions, leek, shallots, lemon grass, curry paste and reserved stock to the pan and bring to a simmer. Reduce the heat, cover the pan tightly and cook gently for 2 minutes. Add the lobster tails, cover the pan again and cook for 2 minutes more. Add the butter pieces and swirl them in, stirring constantly just until the sauce is emulsified, slightly thickened and glossy. Remove from the heat, season to taste with salt and white pepper and stir in the mint.

Assembly

2 tablespoons extra virgin olive oil
1 pound pea tendrils (if unavailable, use baby spinach leaves)

In a medium sauté pan, heat the oil over medium heat. Add the pea tendrils or spinach and toss gently for 1 to 2 minutes, or just until wilted. In 4 heated serving bowls, mound a quarter of the pea tendrils. Spoon some of the lobster, with its sauce, into each bowl.

SOMMELIER'S WINE CHOICE
Coche–Dury Meursault "Les Chevaliéres" (White Burgundy, Côte de Beaune)
Sauzet Puligny–Montrachet "Combettes" (White Burgundy, Côte de Beaune)

John Dory with Truffle Oil

BRAISED ONIONS, SALSIFY AND BITTER GREENS

SERVES 4

This dish was created by former Patina chef Traci Des Jardins, who started with me when she was only 18 years old. White truffle oil is a (relatively) inexpensive way to add the earthy, addictive aroma of white truffles to a dish. It is available in gourmet shops and by mail order (see page 140 for a listing of sources).

Braised Onions

3 tablespoons unsalted butter
3/4 pound pearl onions, peeled
Salt and freshly ground white pepper
1 tablespoon sugar
3 tablespoons white truffle oil
1/2 cup chicken stock (see page 136)

Preheat the oven to 450 degrees F. In a large ovenproof sauté pan, heat the butter over medium heat and add the onions, salt, pepper, sugar and truffle oil. Cook, stirring occasionally, for 4 to 5 minutes, or until slightly colored. Add the stock, cover the pan and roast for 20 to 25 minutes, stirring halfway through the cooking time, until the onions are tender but not falling apart. Drain, reserving the braising liquid, and refrigerate the onions right away to stop the cooking process.

Salsify

1 lemon, juice squeezed
3/4 pound salsify root
1/4 cup unsalted butter
Salt and freshly ground pepper
1/4 cup chicken stock (see page 136)

Fill a medium mixing bowl with cold water and add the lemon and its juice. Peel the salsify and cut into 2-inch lengths on the diagonal, dropping them into the acidulated water as you work. In a large sauté pan, heat the butter over medium heat. Drain and pat the salsify dry, add it to the pan and sauté, turning occasionally so that all sides cook evenly, for 3 to 4 minutes, or just until it begins to brown. Season to taste with salt and pepper and add the chicken stock. Braise the salsify in the pan until it is just tender, about 5 minutes, stirring occasionally. Remove from the heat and set aside while you cook the fish.

Fish

2 tablespoons extra virgin olive oil
4 John Dory fillets with the skin on, about 6 ounces each
Salt and freshly ground white pepper

In a large heavy sauté pan over medium-high heat, heat the oil until very hot. Season the fish with salt and pepper. Add the fish, skin side down, to the pan and sauté for 2 minutes, then turn to the other side and cook for another 2 minutes. Reduce the heat to medium-low, cover and continue to cook for 1 additional minute, or until the fish is browned and firm outside but medium inside. Set aside, covered, while you finish the vegetables.

Assembly

1 teaspoon sherry vinegar
2 teaspoons white truffle oil
2 tablespoons finely chopped Italian (flat-leaf) parsley
1 tablespoon extra virgin olive oil
1 cup firmly packed baby kale leaves
1 cup firmly packed mustard greens
1 cup firmly packed arugula
1 cup firmly packed beet greens

Add the braised onions with their braising liquid to the pan of salsify and reheat gently together. Stir in the vinegar, truffle oil and parsley and remove from the heat.

In a medium sauté pan, heat the olive oil over medium heat. Add all the greens to the pan and toss gently together for 1 to 2 minutes, or just until the greens have wilted. On each of 4 heated large dinner plates, mound some of the salsify mixture and top with a filet of John Dory. Mound some of the greens on top of the fish.

SOMMELIER'S WINE CHOICE
Forman Chardonnay (Napa Valley)
Harrison Chardonnay (Napa Valley)

Lobster Risotto
WITH LOBSTER BOLOGNESE

SERVES 4

Everyone knows the traditional Italian meat sauce, Bolognese. My version is a little different. "Brunoise" is a common French culinary term that means finely diced vegetables sautéed and finished with wine – a flavorful base for many classical and modern dishes.

FISH MAIN COURSES

Lobster

4 Maine lobsters, about 1 1/2 pounds each and very much alive

In a large stockpot, bring a generous amount of water to a boil. In batches if necessary, plunge the lobsters into the boiling water, cover the pan and cook for 5 minutes. Set the lobsters aside to drain on paper towels until cool enough to handle, then crack the shells and remove the meat, reserving the shells. Cut the tails into 3/4-inch medallions and shred the claw and arm meat into large chunks. Set the lobster meat aside, covered and refrigerated, until you are ready for the final assembly.

Lobster Jus

The reserved lobster shells, crushed in a muslin bag with a rolling pin
3 tablespoons extra virgin olive oil
1 tablespoon cognac
1 cup dry white wine
2 medium shallots, coarsely chopped
2 cloves garlic, halved
1 sprig fresh thyme
1 tablespoon tomato paste
1 plum tomato, quartered
1 quart lobster stock (see page 137)

Preheat the oven to 400 degrees F. Place the lobster shells in a large roasting pan and drizzle with 2 tablespoons of the oil. Roast the shells for 15 to 20 minutes, stirring once or twice during the cooking time, until they are bright red and beginning to caramelize. Remove from the oven and add the cognac and wine to the roasting pan. Deglaze, stirring and scraping the bottom and sides of the pan to release all the flavorful bits into the liquid. Set aside.

In a large, heavy saucepan, heat the remaining tablespoon of oil over medium heat. Add the shallots and sauté, stirring occasionally, for 3 to 4 minutes, or until softened. Add the roasted shells with their deglazing liquid, the garlic and thyme and cook, stirring, for 5 minutes. Add the tomato paste and plum tomato and cook for an additional 2 minutes, then add the lobster stock and enough water to cover the shells by 1 inch and bring the mixture to a boil. Reduce the heat and simmer for 1 hour, skimming off fats and impurities as necessary. Strain the stock through a strainer lined with a double

thickness of slightly dampened cheesecloth into a small saucepan, pressing down hard on the solids to extract their flavor. Discard the solids. Over medium-high heat, reduce the stock by half, until only about 3/4 cup of rich and syrupy liquid remains. Set aside, covered, at the back of the stove until you are ready to assemble the dish.

Brunoise

1 tablespoon extra virgin olive oil
1 baby carrot, cut into 1/4-inch dice
3 medium shallots, cut into 1/4-inch dice
1 rib celery, strings removed, cut into 1/4-inch dice
1 small leek, white part only, cut into 1/4-inch dice
2 tablespoons dry white wine

In a large heavy sauté pan, heat the oil over medium heat. Add the diced vegetables and, stirring frequently, cook for 3 to 4 minutes, or until softened (do not allow them to brown). Add the wine to the pan and deglaze, stirring and scraping the bottom and sides to release the flavorful bits into the liquid. Remove from the heat and set aside.

Lobster Bolognese

4 tablespoons extra virgin olive oil
2 medium shallots, finely chopped
1 sprig fresh thyme
2 cloves garlic, finely chopped
10 ripe plum tomatoes, peeled, seeded and coarsely chopped (about 2 cups)
Reserved arm, claw and tail meat from the lobsters
1 tablespoon basil chiffonade (see page 139)
Salt and freshly ground white pepper

In a large sauté pan, heat 2 tablespoons of the oil over medium heat and add the shallots and thyme. Cook the shallots, stirring occasionally, for 3 to 4 minutes, or until softened. Add the garlic and cook for 1 minute more. Add the tomatoes, reduce the heat to medium-low and cook, stirring occasionally, for about 25 minutes, or until the tomatoes have melted and thickened. Add the brunoise, the remaining oil and the reserved lobster meat and stir until heated through. Remove from the heat and add the basil and salt and pepper to taste. Set aside, covered, while you cook the risotto. *(continued on next page)*

Risotto

1 tablespoon extra virgin olive oil
2 medium shallots, finely chopped
1 cup Arborio or other short-grain rice
1/2 cup dry white wine
2 1/2 cups very hot chicken stock (see page 136)
3/4 cup (3 ounces) freshly grated Parmesan cheese
1/4 cup unsalted butter, at room temperature, cut into 4 pieces
Salt and freshly ground white pepper

In a large heavy saucepan, heat the oil over medium heat. Add the shallots and sauté, stirring occasionally, for 3 to 4 minutes, or until softened. Add the rice and stir for 1 to 2 minutes, until it is well coated with the oil and slightly parched. Add the wine and bring to a simmer, then cook for about 3 minutes, until no liquid is left. Begin to add the stock, about 1/2 cup at a time, stirring almost constantly and regulating the heat so that the stock simmers but does not boil. As soon as the previous addition of stock has been absorbed, add more and continue stirring and adding stock until the rice is al dente. The whole process should take about 18 to 20 minutes. Stir in the cheese and add the butter, piece by piece, stirring until absorbed, and season to taste with salt and pepper. Remove from the heat.

Assembly

The reserved lobster jus
1/3 cup unsalted butter, at room temperature, cut into 3 pieces
1 teaspoon finely chopped chives
Salt and freshly ground white pepper
The reserved lobster Bolognese

Bring the pan of lobster jus to a simmer over medium-high heat and swirl in the butter, a piece at a time, stirring and swirling until just emulsified. Remove from the heat, stir in the chives and season to taste with salt and pepper. Gently reheat the lobster Bolognese.

In each of 4 heated serving bowls, mound some of the risotto. Top with a portion of lobster Bolognese and spoon a little of the lobster jus over the top.

SOMMELIER'S WINE CHOICE
Drouhin Pinot Noir (Oregon)
Gouges Nuits St. Georges (Red Burgundy, Côte de Nuits)

Odd Potato Plaques

WITH SALMON IN LASAGNA FORM WITH LITTLENECK CLAM "VINAIGRETTE"

SERVES 4

Perfectly rectangular, 1/8-inch-thick slices of potato for the lasagne come from very large potatoes – the ones we use at Patina average about 1 3/4 pounds apiece.

Clams

1/4 cup extra virgin olive oil
6 medium shallots, thinly sliced
1 sprig fresh thyme
3 pounds littleneck clams, thoroughly scrubbed to remove grit
2 cups dry white wine

In a large saucepan or stockpot, heat the oil over medium heat. Add the shallots and thyme and sauté for 2 to 3 minutes, or until softened. Increase the heat to high and add the clams and the wine. Cover and cook for 4 to 6 minutes, or until all the clams have opened, shaking the pan occasionally while holding the top on to distribute the clams evenly. Remove from the heat and discard any clams that do not open. When the clams are cool enough to handle, remove them from their shells and discard the shells (or if preferred, leave the clams in their shells). Into a medium saucepan, strain the cooking liquid through a colander lined with a double thickness of slightly dampened cheesecloth and reserve the clams in their cooking liquid.

Brunoise

1 tablespoon extra virgin olive oil
1 baby carrot, cut into 1/4-inch dice
3 medium shallots, cut into 1/4-inch dice
1 rib celery, strings removed, cut into 1/4-inch dice
1 small leek, white part only, cut into 1/4-inch dice
2 tablespoons dry white wine

In a large heavy sauté pan, heat the oil over medium heat. Add the diced vegetables and, stirring frequently, cook for 3 to 4 minutes, or until softened (do not allow them to brown). Add the wine to the pan and deglaze, stirring and scraping the bottom and sides to release the flavorful bits into the liquid. Remove from the heat and set aside.

SOMMELIER'S WINE CHOICE
Herrenweg Tokay d'Alsace (Pinot Gris, Alsace)
Domaine Rollin Pernand Vergelesses (Red Burgundy, Côte de Beaune)

Lasagna

1/2 cup unsalted butter, melted
Salt and freshly ground white pepper
2 very large Idaho potatoes, peeled and trimmed into 3 3/4-by-2 1/2-inch blocks
1 1/2 pounds fresh salmon fillet, in one piece

Preheat the oven to 350 degrees F. Line a baking sheet with parchment paper, brush it with some of the butter and sprinkle with a little salt and pepper. With a mandoline or a sharp knife, cut the potato blocks carefully crosswise into 1/8-inch-thick rectangles and arrange them in a single layer on the baking sheet (you should have at least 16 slices). Brush the slices with butter and sprinkle with a little more salt and pepper. Bake them for 10 to 12 minutes, or until just tender, then set aside to cool.

Slice the salmon thinly on the diagonal so that you have twelve 1/4-inch slices as close in size as possible to the potato rectangles. Place the 12 slices of salmon on top of and parallel to 12 of the potato rectangles. You should have 4 potato slices remaining.

Assembly

2 tablespoons extra virgin olive oil
1 cup fresh spinach, stems removed, cut into 1/2-inch-wide strips
2 teaspoons finely chopped Italian (flat-leaf) parsley
Salt and freshly ground black pepper

Preheat the oven to 400 degrees F. Using a slotted spoon, remove the clams from their cooking liquid and set aside briefly. Add the brunoise and the oil to the liquid in the pan and bring to a simmer over medium heat. Cook for 1 minute, add the spinach, then return the clams to the pan. Cook the mixture, stirring frequently, until the spinach has melted into the sauce. Remove the clam juice from the heat and stir in the parsley.

Season the 12 salmon-potato "sandwiches" to taste with salt and pepper and place the baking sheet in the hot oven. Cook for 2 to 3 minutes, or until the salmon is medium-rare. Remove from the oven and on each of 4 heated appetizer plates, make a lasagna out of 3 of the salmon-potato sandwiches, then top each of the lasagne with one of the plain potato slices. Each lasagna should have 3 layers of salmon and 4 layers of potato. Spoon some of the clam vinaigrette along the tops of the lasagne.

Sea Bass

WITH CREAMY LENTILS AND GARLIC INFUSION

SERVES 4

There is unexpected balance in this dish of crisp, grilled fish on its bed of hearty lentils. Save the extra garlic purée for stirring into mashed potatoes or soups, and keep in mind that the lentils must be soaked overnight.

FISH MAIN COURSES

Quadruple-Blanched Garlic Purée

20 cloves garlic, peeled
1/2 cup heavy cream

Place the garlic in a small saucepan filled with cold water and bring to a simmer over medium heat. Simmer for 2 minutes, then drain and return to the same pan and cover with cold water again. Bring to a simmer for 2 minutes and drain again. Repeat the process twice more, then return the drained cloves to the pan and add the cream. Bring to a simmer over low heat and cook for 5 minutes, stirring frequently so that the cream does not scorch or separate. There should be just enough cream to bind the garlic together.

Purée the mixture in a food processor or blender for 2 minutes, scraping down the sides of the bowl as necessary, until very smooth. Push the purée through a fine sieve and set aside. This makes 3/4 cup of purée.

Pearl Onions and Baby Carrots

1 tablespoon extra virgin olive oil
12 pearl onions, peeled
1 tablespoon granulated sugar
Salt and freshly ground white pepper
1/2 cup chicken stock (see page 136)
12 baby carrots, peeled and 1/4 inch of green top left on

In a small sauté pan, heat the oil over medium-high heat and add the onions, sugar and salt and pepper. Cook for 5 to 7 minutes, or until golden, stirring frequently. Add the stock and simmer, stirring occasionally, until the onions are tender, about 7 minutes. Set aside, covered.

In a medium saucepan, bring a generous amount of water to a boil. Plunge the carrots into the water and blanch for 2 to 3 minutes, then refresh them under cold running water and drain on a tea towel.

Lentils

2 slices apple-smoked bacon or other smoky bacon, one slice left whole and the other cut into thin crosswise strips (lardons)
1 small carrot, finely diced
1/2 small onion, finely diced
1 clove garlic, finely chopped
1 sprig fresh thyme
1 tablespoon unsalted butter
3/4 cup small green lentils (French Puy lentils, if available) or standard brown lentils, soaked overnight in water to cover
2 to 3 cups chicken stock (see page 136)

In a large heavy saucepan over medium-low heat, sweat the whole slice of bacon and the lardons just until they have rendered their fat. Remove, drain and reserve the lardons of bacon for the final assembly, leaving the whole slice of bacon in the pan. Add the diced carrot, onion, garlic, thyme and butter and cook the vegetables slowly for 4 to 5 minutes, or until they are tender. Add the lentils and enough stock to cover them by 1 inch. Bring the liquid to a simmer and cook for about 35 minutes, until the lentils are tender, skimming off any impurities that rise to the top. Remove the whole slice of bacon and the thyme.

Sea Bass

4 pieces of sea bass fillet with the skin on, about 6 ounces each
2 tablespoons all-purpose flour
1/4 cup extra virgin olive oil
2 tablespoons unsalted butter
Salt and freshly ground white pepper

Score the skin of the bass in a crisscross pattern. Dust the skin side only with the flour, shaking off the excess. In a large sauté pan, heat the oil and butter over medium-high heat. When they are very hot, sear the fish, skin side down, for 3 to 4 minutes, until golden brown and crisp. Turn the fish to the other side, reduce the heat and cook about 4 minutes more, until the fish is cooked to medium. Season with salt and pepper. Cover with aluminum foil and set aside while you finish the dish. *(continued on next page)*

Croutons

4 thin slices of country-style white bread
2 tablespoons extra virgin olive oil
1 teaspoon finely chopped fresh thyme

Preheat the oven to 400 degrees F. Arrange the bread slices on a baking sheet, brush them with the oil and sprinkle with the thyme. Toast in the oven for 3 to 4 minutes, or until golden, watching carefully to see that they do not burn.

Assembly

The reserved lentils
1/4 cup of the reserved garlic purée
The reserved lardons of bacon
2 scallions, thinly sliced on the diagonal
The reserved onions and carrots
1/3 cup unsalted butter, at room temperature
1 tablespoon basil chiffonade (see page 139)
1 tablespoon finely chopped chives
Salt and freshly ground white pepper

Gently reheat the fish in a warm oven, if necessary. Over medium heat, reheat the lentils and add the garlic purée, lardons, scallions, braised pearl onions with their braising liquid and blanched carrots. Stir gently to mix and, when heated through, stir in the butter until the mixture is just creamy. Remove from the heat, add the basil and chives and season to taste with salt and pepper.

Divide the lentil mixture among 4 heated large dinner plates and place a piece of fish on the top, skin side up. Place a crouton jauntily half on and half off the fish.

SOMMELIER'S WINE CHOICE
Calera Chardonnay "Mt. Harlan Vineyards" (Central Coast)
Arrowood Chardonnay (Sonoma)

Seared Whitefish

WITH FRENCH FRIES "NOT FRIED," ROASTED GARLIC CLOVES AND BRANDADE

SERVES 4

Have you ever had poached french fries? Did you ever imagine that a sauce made from potato water could be so tasty? This recipe's variation of the classic "brandade de morue" is made with fresh fish instead of salt cod, too. Some rules are made to be broken.

Potato Jus

1/4 cup unsalted butter
1 Idaho potato, peeled and cut into
  1/2-inch cubes
1 onion, cut into 1/2-inch cubes
1 medium leek, white part only, cut
  into 1/2-inch cubes

2 ribs celery, cut into 1/2-inch cubes
4 cloves garlic, unpeeled
1 sprig fresh thyme
1/4 teaspoon whole white peppercorns
2 cups chicken stock (see page 136)

In a large, heavy saucepan, melt the butter over medium-low heat. Add the potato, onion, leek, celery, garlic, thyme and whole peppercorns. Sweat the vegetables slowly, stirring occasionally, for about 20 minutes, or until very soft but not browned. Add the stock, bring to a simmer, partially cover and cook slowly for 45 minutes. (If the stock reduces too much, add up to 1 cup of water to keep the level about the same.) Pass the stock through a fine strainer into a small saucepan, pressing down hard on the solids to extract all their flavor; discard the solids. Over high heat, boil the liquid until reduced to about 1/2 cup, skimming off the fat with a large flat spoon. Set the pan aside, covered, until you are ready to finish the dish.

Brandade

4 ounces whitefish fillet, skin on
2 cups milk
1 large Idaho potato, peeled and quartered
1/4 cup unsalted butter

1/4 cup milk or heavy cream
4 tablespoons Quadruple-Blanched Garlic
  Purée (see page 80)
Salt and freshly ground white pepper

Preheat the oven to 400 degrees F. Place the whitefish in a lightly oiled roasting pan and roast for about 6 minutes, or until firm and cooked through. Remove the skin and mash with a fork until well broken up. Set aside. Place the milk and quartered potatoes in a large saucepan, making up the level with water if necessary so that all the potatoes are covered, and bring to a boil. Cook for 20 to 25 minutes, or until tender. When the potatoes are done, drain them and pass through a food mill or mash thoroughly with a masher or a hand blender (do not use a food processor). Place them in a clean pan.

    In a small saucepan, bring the butter and cream to a boil. Slowly add this mixture to the potatoes, stirring all the time, over low heat. Stir in the mashed whitefish and the garlic purée. Season to taste with salt and pepper, cover and set aside until you are ready to assemble the dish.

SOMMELIER'S WINE CHOICE
Stony Hill Chardonnay (Napa Valley)
Far Niente Chardonnay (Napa Valley)

"French Fries"

1 Idaho potato, peeled and cut into 1/4-inch cubes
1 Idaho potato, peeled and cut into 1/3-inch-by-1/3-inch-by-3 1/2-inch batonnets
  (you should have 16)

In 2 separate saucepans, immerse the 2 different sizes of potato separately in generous amounts of cold water, bringing them both to a boil over medium-high heat. Cook until the potatoes are tender but not falling apart — 4 minutes for the cubes and 6 minutes for the batonnets. Remove the pans from the heat and allow to cool. Drain the potato cubes well and add them to the reserved potato jus. Drain the batonnets and set them aside on a lightly buttered baking sheet for the final assembly.

Whitefish

1/4 cup extra virgin olive oil
Four 4-ounce portions whitefish fillet, skin on

2 tablespoons all-purpose flour
Salt and freshly ground white pepper

Preheat the oven to 400 degrees F. In a large ovenproof sauté pan, heat the oil over medium-high heat. On a plate, blend together the flour and salt and pepper to taste. Lightly coat the skin side of the fish fillets with the flour mixture and shake off any excess. When the oil is very hot, fry the fish, skin side down, for 4 minutes, or until the skin is dark brown and crispy. Turn the fish to the other side and place the pan in the oven to finish cooking for 2 to 3 minutes, or until the fish is firm. Leave the oven on; set the fish aside at the back of the stove, uncovered, while you finish the sauce and garnish.

Assembly

1/3 cup extra virgin olive oil
2 tablespoons finely chopped chives

Salt and freshly ground white pepper

Reheat the baking sheet of potato batonnets for about 3 minutes, or until hot. Bring the potato jus to a simmer, add the oil and bring to a fast boil, stirring, so that the oil emulsifies with the jus. Remove from the heat, add the chives and season to taste with salt and white pepper. Gently reheat the brandade, if necessary.

    On each of 4 large heated dinner plates, mound some of the brandade in the center and top with a fillet of whitefish, skin side up. Place 4 batonnets in a square around each serving and spoon a little of the sauce, with its potato cubes, over each of the "fries."

Roasted Middle Piece of Halibut
WITH FRESH HORSERADISH BUTTER

SERVES 4

Halibut is all too often overcooked, dry and disappointing. Cooking a steak with the bone in rather than a fillet makes it easier to keep the fish moist, and the middle piece of the fish is the tenderest and juiciest of all.

Garniture

1/2 cup duck fat or clarified butter (see page 136)
8 very small red or white rose potatoes, sliced 1/4 inch thick
2 medium shallots, finely chopped
1 clove garlic, finely chopped
2 cups spinach, stems removed, cut into 1-inch strips
Salt and freshly ground white pepper

In a sauté pan just large enough to hold all the potatoes in one layer, heat the duck fat or clarified butter over medium-high heat until very hot. Add the potatoes and sauté, turning occasionally to cook all sides evenly, for 5 to 7 minutes, or until golden brown and cooked through. Reduce the heat to medium and add the shallots and garlic. Cook, stirring occasionally, for 2 minutes more, then add the spinach and toss all together just until the spinach has wilted. Season to taste with salt and pepper and set aside.

Halibut

4 halibut steaks, bone in (8 to 10 ounces each)
Salt and freshly ground white pepper
2 tablespoons all-purpose flour
2 tablespoons unsalted butter

Preheat the oven to 400 degrees F. Season the steaks with salt and pepper to taste and sprinkle the flour evenly on both sides, shaking off any excess. In a large ovenproof sauté pan, heat the butter over medium-high heat. When the pan is very hot, add the steaks and sauté for 3 to 4 minutes, or until one side is golden brown. Turn the steaks to the other side and put the pan in the hot oven to finish cooking for 5 to 6 minutes, depending on the thickness of the steaks, or until they are medium-rare and opaque.

Assembly

The reserved potato garniture
3/4 cup unsalted butter, at room temperature, cut into 6 pieces
2 tablespoons grated fresh horseradish
1 tablespoon finely chopped Italian (flat-leaf) parsley

Gently reheat the potato garniture, if necessary. On each of 4 large heated dinner plates, mound some of the potato mixture and place a halibut steak on the top. In a small saucepan, heat the butter over medium heat and cook, swirling the pan, until it turns a deep brown-tinged gold (this is called beurre noisette because it is cooked to the color of hazelnuts). Do not allow it to darken and burn; remove it immediately from the heat. Stir in the horseradish and parsley and spoon some of the sauce over each of the steaks.

SOMMELIER'S WINE CHOICE
Matanzas Creek Chardonnay (Sonoma)
Cambria Chardonnay "Katherine's Vineyard" (Santa Maria)

Peppered Tournedos of Tuna
WITH BOK CHOY AND PONZU SAUCE

SERVES 4

This is a Patina classic, born in 1989, appreciated and imitated ever since. Ponzu sauce is a mixture of soy sauce and citrus flavors that is sometimes available in Japanese markets; it is much better made up from scratch each time, however.

Wonton Skin Garnish

12 sheets wonton skins, cut into 1/4-inch strips
Vegetable oil for deep-frying

Pull the wonton strips apart, as they will tend to stick to one another when you cut them. In a large, heavy saucepan or deep-fryer, heat the oil to 375 degrees F. Using a skimmer, plunge the wonton strips into the hot oil and cook for 15 to 20 seconds, or until golden. Drain on paper towels. When they are cool enough to handle but still quite warm, gently press the strips into 4 loose balls and set aside.

Tuna

2 tablespoons coarsely cracked black pepper
1 1/4 pounds best-quality ahi tuna fillet, in one piece

Spread the cracked pepper evenly on a tray or baking sheet with sides. Roll the tuna fillet in the pepper to form a fairly even crust. Set aside, covered, at room temperature.

Ponzu Sauce

2 tablespoons low-sodium soy sauce
2 tablespoons lemon juice
1 teaspoon grated fresh ginger
2 tablespoons chicken stock (see page 136)
Pinch freshly ground black pepper
2 tablespoons extra virgin olive oil

In a medium saucepan over medium heat, combine the soy sauce, lemon juice, ginger, stock, pepper and oil. Bring just to a boil and immediately remove from the heat.

Cooking and Assembly

4 large leaves of bok choy or 8 baby bok choy, ends trimmed, halved lengthwise
The reserved tuna fillet
4 whole scallions, root ends trimmed, for the garnish
1 tablespoon finely chopped scallion, white and light green part only, for the sauce
1 small garlic clove, finely chopped
1 plum tomato, peeled, seeded and diced (see page 139)

Preheat the oven to 400 degrees F. In the top of a steamer over simmering water, steam the bok choy until it is tender, about 5 to 6 minutes. Heat an ovenproof nonstick skillet over high heat. When the skillet is very hot, sear the tuna and whole scallions, turning the scallions after 15 seconds and removing them when they are browned on both sides. Sear the tuna fillet for a total of 4 minutes, turning with kitchen tongs and a spatula so that all 4 sides are equally seared. Put the pan in the hot oven to finish cooking for 2 to 3 minutes, or until medium-rare. Remove from the oven and, using a very sharp knife, slice the fillet into 8 equal pieces.

Gently reheat the Ponzu sauce and stir in the chopped scallion, garlic and tomato. Mound some of the bok choy onto 4 heated large dinner plates. Top with 2 of the tuna tournedos per serving, then spoon a little of the warm sauce over the tuna. Garnish each plate with a grilled whole scallion.

SOMMELIER'S WINE CHOICE
Babcock Sauvignon Blanc (Santa Barbara)
Spottswoode Sauvignon Blanc (Napa Valley)

EARLY SATURDAY NIGHT, FRONT OF THE HOUSE

7 p.m.

Patina has been open for an hour and a half, but most people who came in early were picking up boxed dinners to take with them to a concert at the Hollywood Bowl. The few seated diners were also on their way somewhere else and ordered like the lunch crowd, something quick.

Early evenings are always slow. The waiters' meeting was held, as usual, at 5:50 p.m. — unthinkable if the place had been busy. The first dirty dish didn't have to be taken to the kitchen until 6:30. Three of the six front waiters stood around at the back wall in their white shirts and neckties, talking about drinks: "Does that need an onion?" Most diners were still studying their menus, not ready to order anything but *cocktails*.

"Ordering, please. Bloody Mary 98, vodka rocks." Chris, the bartender, writes the order down so that the waiter can add it to the table's bill at the end of the meal. Silver platters are stacked on the bar by the computer, and each one is already covered with a cloth napkin, for delivering drink orders. They're handy for pickup, but kind of get in the way when waiters are trying to punch in their orders.

Dinner is a more serious affair than lunch. The menu is much longer, and the waiter has more specials to explain. "For an appetizer," one tells a couple in their early 30s, "we have *Santa Barbara shrimp* à la niçoise; also a truffle risotto, and rabbit kidneys with *pearl onions*, carrots and roasted croutons. For an entrée we have braised veal shanks with baby vegetables, veal loin with two potato preparations, and

"

When I was 23, I was the sous-chef at the Hotel Negresco in Nice in a kitchen with 40 other employees, and
I was the only foreigner there. It helped me a lot to be determined and ambitious.

"

EARLY SATURDAY NIGHT, FRONT OF THE HOUSE

the fish of the evening is roasted sea bass with carrots and clam juice. It may be too early to think about dessert, but I'd like to mention that tonight we have fresh California-grown *fraises de bois*."

Unobtrusively, he slips a heavy bookbound wine list onto the table and retires. The man marvels at some of the dishes, reading their names aloud, and several times flips through the wine list for ideas. The woman has been here before. Her eyes light up: "Here's that lobster thing!" she says.

When waiters get food orders, they punch them in at a computer terminal, and a copy of the orders immediately prints out in the kitchen. They put in their personal ID code, the ID number of the table, dish codes (appetizers first, then entrées, all identified with each diner's position at the table), then wine codes. Dessert orders are added at the end of the meal. The waiters have memorized most of the dish codes, but the **several hundred wine codes need looking up.**

"I need a champagne," says a waiter to Chris at 7:00 p.m. on the dot. "How many are we doing tonight?"

"I hear we've got 192 on the book," Chris says.

People are arriving steadily, and the dining room is almost full. A hostess tries to mollify two customers who don't want to sit in the bar, even though they'd have a booth. Gary, the maître d', finds them a table in another room. A party of 14 has reserved a private room for the evening; they're still straggling in.

"Two Mumm champagnes and a Crown on the rocks, please."

"Ordering, please. One pinot noir."

"Ordering, please. One framboise, but I need you to put it in two glasses."

" In California, everybody loves innovation. But in Europe, the older restaurants have specialties that have stood the test of time, and that's what you go to them for. That should be part of what we do. "

My own style I call classic with an edge. I like people to be intrigued
by the whimsicality of the menu, but dazzled by the food.

7:15 p.m.

The tempo continues to pick up. Waiters and hostesses pause on their errands to advise each other about the tastes of particular customers. Wineglasses are being whisked off to a washing machine that is reserved exclusively for them.

At the bar Chris is swirling ice cubes around a glass to chill it before pouring in *Stolichnaya* from a bottle stored in the freezer. "You got all the grappas?" a waiter asks.

"I'm out of the fragola," Chris says. "But I've got a really good new one." He nods toward a strikingly designed bottle of *Italian brandy* that's on the shelf with the vintage Armagnacs and single-malt Scotches. "It's raspberry." The Stoli is at freezing temperature, and it pours into the glass with an almost syrupy consistency.

7:30 p.m. Dining rooms are almost full, conversation level approaching a dull roar. The waiters move at a trot as soon as they're at a discreet distance from the tables they're serving.

"Ordering, please. Ramos Fizz."

"That takes 20 minutes."

"She wants something with just this much alcohol," the waiter says, practically pinching his fingers together. "She just likes the fizzy part."

EARLY SATURDAY NIGHT, FRONT OF THE HOUSE

"Well, it's not going to taste like a Ramos Fizz."

"Can you just make her something?"

Heard through the kitchen door, the usual cries. **"Pick up 14 on 4."** There's trouble in the kitchen, though.

A waiter ordering four appetizers on the computer accidentally inserted a line after the first two. To the kitchen, a line on the printout means the end of an order, so only two appetizers were made. The waiter can't serve just half the party, so now all four diners will have to wait, wondering why, while all four appetizers are made again from scratch.

The humiliated waiter hunches over his flawed order sheet, trying to burn the error into his brain. **Joachim** quietly tells him, "Mistakes like this cannot happen." He turns to Jonny. "There are four people sitting there with nothing to eat. Send them something to keep them happy."

For once, Jonny doesn't say "Yes, sir," but only nods.

By 7:45 p.m. the place is about full, and the waiters are bringing orders for *espresso* and *cappuccino* as the first main seating of the night prepares to leave. Now there's a small crowd at the bar, including people who study the menu as they wait for their tables.

Real Slow-Roasted Veal Shank

WITH CALIFORNIA BABY VEGETABLES AND HAND-PICKED CHANTERELLES

SERVES 4

People seem to ignore braising as a cooking technique these days, forgetting that it produces wonderful, flavorful, family-style dishes such as this one.
The meat will be so tender it will just fall from the bone.

Veal Shank

2 teaspoons extra virgin olive oil
One 4- to 5-pound veal shank
Salt and freshly ground black pepper
1 medium carrot, coarsely chopped
2 ribs celery, coarsely chopped
1/2 medium yellow onion, coarsely chopped

2 cloves garlic, coarsely chopped
1 sprig of fresh thyme
4 plum tomatoes, peeled, seeded and coarsely chopped (see page 139)
1/4 cup white wine
2 cups chicken stock (see page 136)

In a large sauté pan, heat the oil over high heat. Using heavy kitchen tongs and a carving fork to steady the meat, sear the veal shank evenly for about 6 to 7 minutes, or until all sides are golden brown. Season the shank with salt and pepper to taste and remove it to a large braising pan or oval Dutch oven. Set aside. Meanwhile, preheat the oven to 325 degrees F. Add the carrot, celery and onion to the sauté pan and reduce the heat to medium. Cook the vegetables, stirring occasionally to prevent them from burning, for 8 to 10 minutes, or until golden. Add the garlic, thyme and tomatoes and cook for 1 minute more, stirring, until the garlic releases its aroma. Add the wine to the pan and deglaze, stirring and scraping the bottom and sides so that all the flavorful bits are released into the liquid. Add the stock, stir to mix well and pour the mixture over the veal shank in the braising pan. Cover the pan and braise in the hot oven for 2 1/2 to 3 hours, basting the shank with the liquid every 10 to 15 minutes and turning the shank over every 30 minutes. When done, the meat should be very tender. Remove the shank to an ovenproof platter, cover and set aside. Strain the braising juices into a large saucepan, discarding the solids. Over high heat, reduce the braising liquid by about three-quarters, skimming off the fats and impurities as you do so, and set it aside, covered.

Baby Vegetables

1/4 pound baby carrots, peeled and tops trimmed to 1/4 inch
1/4 pound baby turnips, washed
1/4 pound tiny haricots verts
1/4 pound thin asparagus, trimmed and bottom 1 inch of stalk peeled
1/2 pound Yukon Gold or other waxy potato such as white rose, peeled and cut into quarters
1/4 pound cherry tomatoes
1 cup fresh peas (about 1/2 pound in their pods)
1/4 pound fresh fava beans, blanched for 2 minutes in boiling water and shells removed (optional)
1/4 pound fresh spinach leaves, stems removed

Have ready a large bowl of ice water. In a large saucepan, bring a generous amount of water to a boil. Using a skimmer, blanch the vegetables individually by plunging them into the boiling water and cooking for 1 to 4 minutes, depending on their size, or until al dente. Remove each vegetable with the skimmer and plunge it into the ice water for 1 minute (you may need to add more ice to the water halfway through the blanching process). Drain the vegetables on a tea towel. Proceed until all the vegetables have been blanched, chilled and drained.

Chanterelles

1 tablespoon unsalted butter
1 small shallot, finely chopped
4 ounces fresh chanterelles, or other wild mushrooms of your choice, wiped clean
Salt and freshly ground white pepper

In a small sauté pan, melt the butter over medium heat. Add the shallot and cook, stirring occasionally, for 3 to 4 minutes, or until softened. Add the chanterelles and cook for 4 to 5 minutes, stirring occasionally, until tender. Season to taste with salt and pepper.

Assembly

2 tablespoons unsalted butter, at room temperature, cut into 2 pieces
2 tablespoons finely chopped chives

If the veal shank has cooled too much, reheat it, covered with foil, in a 350-degree F oven for 10 to 15 minutes, or until heated through. Return the reduced braising liquid to a simmer and swirl in the butter, a piece at a time, stirring and swirling until just absorbed and the sauce is glossy. Add all the baby vegetables and the chanterelles to the saucepan and toss them gently until they are heated through and coated with the sauce. Place the veal shank in the center of a large heated oval serving platter. Remove the vegetables from the sauce with a slotted spoon and arrange them all around the shank. Drizzle the remaining sauce over the shank and sprinkle the chives over all.

SOMMELIER'S WINE CHOICE
Corison Cabernet Sauvignon (Napa Valley)
Von Strasser Cabernet Sauvignon "Diamond Mountain" (Napa Valley)

Everything from a Rabbit

WITH POLENTA GNOCCHI AND ZUCCHINI MOUSSE

Restaurants only use the saddle of the rabbit. One day I just decided to use everything – ribs, legs, liver, everything. People always expect gnocchi to be made from potatoes, but at the restaurant, we do a number of unexpected gnocchi dishes fashioned from everything from wild rice and shrimp to sweet potato and ginger. Here's a variation using polenta.

Rabbit and Jus

2 rabbits, jointed to yield the following: 4 rear legs, 4 loins with the flaps attached, 4 ribs,
    4 forelegs, 2 carcasses, 2 livers and 2 kidneys
4 medium shallots, coarsely chopped
1 medium carrot, coarsely chopped
4 unpeeled cloves garlic, crushed with a chef's knife
1/2 cup white wine
1 sprig fresh thyme
2 cups chicken stock (see page 136)

Preheat the oven to 400 degrees F. Remove the bones from the rabbits' rear legs. Roll the loins up inside the flaps and secure with toothpicks in 3 places on each loin. Cut each loin into 3 "mini rolls," each one secured with a toothpick. Wrap all the rabbit parts except the carcasses in plastic wrap and refrigerate them while you make the jus. In a large roasting pan, combine the rabbit carcasses with the shallots, carrot and garlic and roast in the hot oven for 20 to 25 minutes, turning halfway through the cooking time, until brown and caramelized. Tilt the pan and spoon off and discard any accumulated fat. Reduce the oven heat to 350 degrees F. On top of the stove over medium heat, add the wine and thyme to the pan and deglaze, stirring and scraping the bottom and sides to release all the flavorful bits into the liquid. Reduce until the wine has evaporated almost completely away, then add the stock and simmer, stirring occasionally, until the stock has reduced by about two-thirds and a scant 1 cup of liquid remains. Strain it through a strainer lined with a double thickness of slightly dampened cheesecloth into a small saucepan, pressing down hard on the solids to extract all their flavor. Discard the solids and set the jus aside, covered.

Polenta Gnocchi

1/2 medium Idaho potato, peeled and quartered
1 cup chicken stock
1/2 cup coarse yellow cornmeal or polenta
1/2 cup all-purpose flour
Salt and freshly ground white pepper

Bring a medium saucepan of water to a boil. Add the potato pieces and simmer for 20 to 25 minutes, or until tender. Drain the potatoes and dry them on a baking sheet in the hot oven for 5 minutes. Put the potatoes through a ricer or mash thoroughly with a masher or hand blender. You should have 1 cup of mashed potato. In a large, heavy saucepan, bring the stock to a simmer over medium-high heat. Sprinkle in the cornmeal in a steady stream, whisking all the time in the same direction until it is all blended in and no lumps remain. Reduce the heat to low, switch to a wooden spoon or paddle, and stir every 2 to 3 minutes for about 30 minutes, or until the polenta grains have softened. The mixture should be very thick. In a medium mixing bowl, combine the mashed potato with the polenta, flour and salt and pepper to taste. Stir with a wooden spoon to mix thoroughly and turn the ball of dough (it should be just slightly sticky but not wet) out onto a lightly floured work surface. Form the dough into cylinders about 3/4 inch in diameter and cut the cylinders into 1-inch lengths. Set the gnocchi aside on a floured plate until you are ready to assemble the dish.

Zucchini Mousse

2 slices white bread, crusts removed, torn into small pieces
2 tablespoons heavy cream
1 tablespoon extra virgin olive oil
2 medium zucchini, skin and outermost 1/2 inch of flesh removed in strips all the way around,
    center core discarded, blanched for 2 minutes in boiling water and drained
5 leaves fresh basil
Salt and freshly ground white pepper

In a small bowl, combine the bread with the cream, mash together and set aside. In a medium sauté pan, heat the oil over medium-low heat and sauté the zucchini strips for 2 to 3 minutes, or until al dente. Do not allow to brown. In a food processor fitted with the metal blade, combine the zucchini, basil and bread mixture and process for 20 to 30 seconds, scraping down the sides of the bowl as necessary. Season to taste with salt and pepper and set aside in a small saucepan. *(continued on next page)*

Assembly

2 tablespoons unsalted butter, for cooking the rabbit
The reserved rabbit parts
Salt and freshly ground white pepper
The reserved rabbit jus
1/2 cup unsalted butter at room temperature, cut into 4 pieces, for the sauce
12 small shiitake mushroom caps, sautéed until golden in 1 tablespoon unsalted butter
1 tablespoon finely chopped parsley
The reserved zucchini mousse
The reserved polenta gnocchi

Preheat the oven to 350 degrees F and put a large sauté pan of water on to boil. In another large sauté pan, melt the 2 tablespoons of butter over medium-high heat. Season all the rabbit parts with salt and pepper to taste and sauté the legs, loin rolls, forelegs and ribs on one side for 2 to 3 minutes, or until golden. Turn to the other side and finish cooking in the hot oven for 4 to 5 minutes, or until just done to medium. Remove the parts to an ovenproof plate, cover with aluminum foil, and turn off the oven. In the same pan, sauté the livers and kidneys, turning halfway through the cooking time, for 1 to 2 minutes, or until they are browned on the outside but still pink inside. Add to the plate with the other rabbit parts and place the plate in the turned-off oven with the door ajar. Bring the reserved jus to a simmer and add the butter, a piece at a time, stirring and swirling just until each piece is emulsified before adding the next. Add the shiitake caps and parsley and stir to mix. Remove from the heat and cover. Gently reheat the zucchini mousse over very low heat, stirring so that it does not scorch and is just warmed through. Meanwhile, drop the polenta gnocchi into the sauté pan of boiling water (do not overcrowd them in the pan; you may need to do this in batches) and cook until they rise to the surface, then remove with a slotted spoon, drain briefly on a tea towel and add to the warm mushrooms and jus. On each of 4 heated large dinner plates, mound about 2 tablespoons of the zucchini mousse. Arrange 1 each of the rabbit legs, ribs and forelegs and 3 of the loin rolls around the edge of each plate and place 1 liver or kidney in the center. Spoon some of the warm ragoût of gnocchi and mushrooms in the center, making sure each diner gets 3 shiitake caps.

SOMMELIER'S WINE CHOICE
Cain Five Cabernet Sauvignon (Napa Valley)
Chateau Malescot Bordeaux "Saint Exupery" (Margaux)

Osso Bucco "Summertime"

SERVES 4

These veal shanks are poached rather than braised like a classic Italian osso bucco, and the sauce has a complex flavor that is enriched by its finish of olive oil.
With its garnish of colorful and fresh baby vegetables, this is a very light dish.

Shanks

4 pieces veal shank, cut as for osso bucco,
 about 1 pound each
Salt and freshly ground white pepper
1/2 cup unsalted butter
2 large carrots, coarsely chopped
2 ribs celery, coarsely chopped
1 large yellow onion, coarsely chopped

1 medium leek, white part only, coarsely chopped
3 cloves garlic, peeled
1 sprig fresh thyme
1 teaspoon whole white peppercorns
1 small bay leaf
7 cups chicken stock, or enough to
 cover the shanks (see page 136)

Preheat the oven to 325 degrees F. Tie a piece of string around the outside of each veal shank to keep it from falling apart during cooking; salt and pepper the shanks to taste. In a large braising pan, melt the butter over medium-low heat and add the vegetables, garlic, thyme, peppercorns and bay leaf. Sweat the vegetables for 2 to 3 minutes, but do not allow them to brown. Add the shanks and the stock to the pan (the stock should completely cover the shanks). Bring the broth to a simmer over medium-high heat, cover the pan and place it in the oven. Braise for 1 1/2 to 2 1/2 hours, depending on the size of the shanks, or until the meat is very tender, then remove the shanks to a plate while you strain the cooking broth, pressing down hard on the solids to extract all their flavor; discard the solids. Return half of the broth and all of the shanks to the original pan, cover and set aside. In a clean saucepan, reduce the remaining half of the broth by three -quarters over medium-high heat, skimming the fat and impurities with a large flat spoon as you do so (this may take from 20 to 30 minutes). Set the reduced broth aside until you are ready to assemble the dish.

Vegetables

8 baby carrots, with 1/4 inch of green top left on, peeled
4 baby turnips, quartered
1 1/4 cups haricots verts, halved lengthwise
1 1/4 cups yellow wax beans, halved lengthwise
1/2 cup fava beans, blanched for 2 minutes in boiling water and shells removed
1/4 pound asparagus, tips only
8 baby artichokes, stems snapped off, trimmed of tough outer leaves, top two-thirds of leaves cut
 off, and quartered

Have ready a large bowl of ice water. In a medium saucepan, bring a generous amount of water to a boil. Blanch the carrots, turnips, haricots verts, wax beans, fava beans and asparagus tips, one type of vegetable at a time, and then refresh them briefly in the ice water before draining them on a tea towel. The vegetables should be al dente, and blanching times will range from 2 to 5 minutes, depending on the size of the vegetables. Lastly, blanch the baby artichokes, which will take from 5 to 7 minutes, depending on their size.

Assembly

Kosher or sea salt
The reduced veal broth
1/2 cup extra virgin olive oil
1 red bell pepper, roasted, peeled and cut into 1/4-inch strips (see page 48)
1 yellow bell pepper, roasted, peeled and cut into 1/4-inch strips (see page 48)
8 cherry tomatoes, peeled but with stem left on
2 cups baby spinach, stems removed
2 tablespoons finely chopped Italian (flat-leaf) parsley
Small handful parsley sprigs

Over medium-low heat, reheat the shanks gently in their broth and place 1 in each of 4 heated large serving bowls. (Reserve the broth for another use, such as vegetable soup.) Sprinkle each with a few grains of the coarse salt. Bring the reduced broth to a simmer over high heat, add the oil and then simmer and swirl to emulsify it with the juices for 1 to 2 minutes. Add the blanched vegetables and the red and yellow peppers to the broth and bring it back to a simmer. Add the cherry tomatoes, spinach and parsley and toss to mix. Return to a simmer and spoon some of the vegetables on top of the veal shanks. Snip and remove the strings around the shanks and top with the sprigs of parsley.

SOMMELIER'S WINE CHOICE
Silver Oak Cabernet Sauvignon (Napa Valley)
Duckhorn Cabernet Sauvignon (Napa Valley)

MEAT MAIN COURSES

High Cholesterol Foie Gras

WITH BUTTER POTATO CHIPS AND SQUAB CONFIT SAUCE

SERVES 4

This is gourmet "guy" food – meat and potatoes on a higher level.

Potato Chips

1/4 cup unsalted butter, melted
Salt and freshly ground white pepper, to taste
1 large Idaho potato, peeled and trimmed flat on one long edge to form a beginning surface
  for slicing

Preheat the oven to 400 degrees F. Line 2 baking sheets with parchment paper and brush them with some of the butter, then sprinkle with a little salt and pepper. Using a mandoline, cut the potato carefully lengthwise into paper-thin slices (you should have at least 12). Arrange them in a single layer on the baking sheets, brush well with butter and season again with salt and pepper. Cover each layer with another sheet of parchment paper and top with another baking sheet of the same size to keep the slices lying flat. Bake for 25 to 30 minutes or until golden brown, checking to be sure that the potatoes do not burn and turning the sheets around halfway through the cooking time to help the potatoes brown evenly. Remove the slices from the pan; if they are very oily, drain them briefly on paper towels. Set aside, uncovered, until you are ready to assemble the dish.

Mashed Potatoes

1 large or 2 small Idaho potatoes,   *1/4 cup heavy cream*
  peeled and quartered   *3 tablespoons unsalted butter*
1/4 cup milk   *Salt and freshly ground white pepper*

Bring a medium saucepan of lightly salted water to a boil over high heat and cook the potatoes for about 20 minutes, or until tender, and drain them well. In another saucepan, bring the milk and cream to a boil and add the butter, swirling until it is melted. Press the potatoes through a food mill or a ricer into the saucepan with the milk and butter and stir until well mixed. Season to taste with salt and pepper and set aside, covered.

Squab

1 tablespoon unsalted butter
2 boneless squab breasts, halved lengthwise into 4 single breasts

In a medium sauté pan, heat the butter over medium-high heat. When the butter is hot, sear the squab breasts for 1 minute on each side, then reduce the heat, cover the pan and continue to cook for 2 to 3 minutes, or until medium-rare. Remove to a cutting board and cover the breasts with aluminum foil until you are ready to assemble the dish.

Confit Sauce

1 tablespoon unsalted butter
2 tablespoons finely diced carrot
2 tablespoons finely diced leek
2 tablespoons finely diced celery
1 cup chicken stock (see page 136)

2 legs squab confit, shredded (see page 36),
  or 1/3 cup shredded duck confit
3 tablespoons unsalted butter at room
  temperature, cut into 3 pieces
2 tablespoons finely chopped chives

In a large sauté pan, heat the 1 tablespoon of butter over medium heat. Add the carrot, leek and celery and sauté, stirring occasionally, for 3 to 4 minutes or until softened. In a medium saucepan over medium-high heat, reduce the stock by half, until there is only 1/2 cup remaining. Stir in the diced vegetables and the shredded confit and return to a simmer, then swirl in the butter, a piece at a time, whisking just until emulsified. Remove from the heat and stir in the chives.

Assembly

4 ounces "A" grade duck liver or chicken liver, thinly sliced (you should have 8 slices) (optional)

Preheat the oven to 350 degrees F. Slice each squab breast on the diagonal into two 2-inch-thick slices. On a lightly oiled baking sheet, layer the ingredients as follows: a good dollop of mashed potatoes, a potato chip, more mashed potatoes, a slice of squab breast, sliced duck liver, if desired, mashed potato, etc., until you have 2 layers of everything, ending with a third potato chip as the last layer. Heat the layer cake for 1 to 2 minutes, or until heated through. With a flat-ended metal spatula, carefully transfer each layer cake to the center of a large heated dinner plate, steadying with a finger so that the cakes do not topple over. Spoon a little of the confit sauce around and over each one.

SOMMELIER'S WINE CHOICE
Jerry Luper Cabernet Sauvignon (Napa Valley)
Château Phélan-Ségur Bordeaux (St. Estephe)

Roasted Medallions of Rack of Lamb

WITH FRESH PEAS, PEARL ONIONS, CHANTERELLES AND ROASTED YUKON POTATOES

SERVES 4

This is a dish for when spring turns into summer; when the peas are perfectly fresh, the baby lambs are tender and the mushrooms are at the height of their flavor.

MEAT MAIN COURSES

Lamb Jus

2 whole racks of lamb, about 1 pound each
1 unpeeled head of garlic, halved
1/4 cup extra virgin olive oil
1 medium carrot, coarsely chopped
3 medium shallots, coarsely chopped
1/2 cup white wine
1 sprig fresh thyme
1 small plum tomato, coarsely chopped
1 quart chicken stock (see page 136)

Remove the meat from each rack by scraping the flesh away from the bones in one piece using a sharp boning knife, or have the butcher do this for you. Wrap and refrigerate the lamb loins. You will need the bones to make the sauce. Preheat the oven to 400 degrees F. In a large roasting pan, combine the lamb bones, garlic and oil and toss together. Roast for 15 minutes, turning the mixture over occasionally, then add the carrot and shallots. Toss together and roast for a further 10 to 15 minutes, or until the mixture is browned and beginning to caramelize. Remove the pan from the oven and, pushing the solids to one side, spoon off and discard the excess fat. On top of the stove, add the wine and deglaze the pan, stirring and scraping the bottom and sides to release all the flavorful bits into the liquid. Add the thyme and tomato and reduce the liquid over medium heat until it has evaporated. Add the stock and again reduce the liquid over medium heat until a scant 1 cup remains. Strain the stock through a strainer lined with a double thickness of slightly dampened cheesecloth into a small saucepan, pressing hard on the solids to extract all their flavor. Discard the solids. Reduce the stock again until there is just over 1/2 cup of liquid remaining, and set aside, covered, until you are ready to assemble the dish.

Pearl Onions

1 tablespoon extra virgin olive oil
20 pearl onions, peeled
Salt and freshly ground pepper
1 tablespoon granulated sugar
1/2 cup chicken stock

In a small sauté pan, heat the oil over medium-high heat and add the pearl onions, salt and pepper to taste and sugar. Sauté, stirring occasionally, for 5 to 7 minutes, or until the onions are golden and caramelized. Add the stock and simmer for about 6 more minutes, until they are tender. Remove from the heat and set aside, in their jus.

Chanterelles

1/4 cup unsalted butter
3 medium shallots, finely chopped
10 ounces fresh chanterelle mushrooms or other wild mushroom of your choice
1/2 cup chicken stock (see page 136)

In a large saucepan, heat the butter over medium-low heat. Add the shallots and sweat for 3 to 4 minutes, or until translucent. Add the chanterelles and sweat for about 5 minutes to release some of their juices. Add the stock, which should cover the mushrooms, cover the pan and bring the liquid to a simmer. Simmer over low heat for 5 to 7 minutes, or until the mushrooms are tender; set aside in their jus.

Potatoes

4 large Yukon Gold, white or red rose potatoes or other waxy potatoes, peeled and quartered
1/2 cup clarified butter (see page 136)
Salt and freshly ground white pepper

Using a sharp paring knife, trim the potatoes into barrel shapes about 2 inches long. (Reserve the trimmings for soup or mashed potatoes, if desired.) In a large sauté pan, heat the clarified butter over medium-high heat and when it is very hot, add the potatoes. Turning often, sauté the potatoes for 8 to 10 minutes, or until golden and cooked through. Drain quickly through a sieve to remove the excess butter and set the potatoes aside in a small ovenproof dish. Season to taste with salt and pepper. *(continued on next page)*

Lamb

1 large egg yolk, beaten together with 2 tablespoons extra virgin olive oil
4 slices white bread, lightly toasted and ground into dry bread crumbs in a food processor
2 cloves garlic, finely chopped
1 teaspoon finely chopped Italian (flat-leaf) parsley
Salt and freshly ground white pepper
The reserved lamb loins
1/4 cup unsalted butter
2 cloves unpeeled garlic, crushed with a chef's knife
1 sprig fresh thyme

Preheat the oven to 400 degrees F for the final assembly. Pour the egg and olive oil mixture onto a large plate. On another large plate, mix the bread crumbs with the garlic and parsley, add salt and pepper to taste and toss together well. Roll the lamb loins in the egg mixture, wiping off any excess, then in the breadcrumb mixture, patting the crumbs into the surface so that they adhere well. In a large heavy sauté pan, heat the butter over medium-high heat and add the garlic and thyme. When the foam has subsided and the butter is very hot, add the breaded lamb loins and turn the heat down to very low. Sauté the lamb slowly for about 5 to 7 minutes, turning with kitchen tongs until it is golden brown all over but still rosy pink on the inside. Remove from the pan and allow to rest, covered with aluminum foil, while you finish the ragoût.

Ragoût of Peas and Chanterelles

The reserved pearl onions, with their jus
12 roasted garlic cloves (see page 138)
The reserved cooked chanterelles, with their jus
3/4 cup fresh peas, blanched for 2 minutes in boiling water and drained
1 tablespoon finely chopped Italian (flat-leaf) parsley
Salt and freshly ground white pepper
2 tablespoons unsalted butter

Add the onions with their jus and the roasted garlic to the pan of chanterelles with their jus and bring back up to a simmer over low heat. Add the peas, parsley, salt and pepper to taste and the butter and bring up to a simmer again, stirring constantly, until the mixture is warmed through and glossy. Cover the pan.

Assembly

The reserved potatoes
The reserved lamb jus
2 tablespoons unsalted butter

Gently reheat the potatoes in the hot oven for 3 minutes, or until heated through. Bring the lamb jus to a simmer over low heat and swirl in the butter, stirring and swirling until it is absorbed and the sauce is glossy. On each of 4 heated large dinner plates, mound some of the warm ragoût. Slice each lamb loin into 6 medallions and place 3 of them atop each serving. Surround the ragoût with the barrel potatoes and spoon some of the sauce over the top.

SOMMELIER'S WINE CHOICE
Niebaum-Coppola Cabernet Sauvignon (Napa Valley)
Château Gruaud-Larose Bordeaux (Saint-Julien)

> 66
> We take an intellectual approach to food. A dish has to have integrity and flavor, and it all has to come together in a ten-second period.
> 99

Venison Medallions
WITH PERSIMMONS AND CELERY ROOT MOUSSE WITH BLACK PEPPER SAUCE

SERVES 4

*Ask your butcher to remove the venison loin from the bones and chop the bones up for the stock. You will need to start with about a
3-pound loin, with the bone in, to yield a 1 1/4-pound boneless loin, which can then be trimmed into 8 equal medallions. If you slice the celery root with a mandoline,
the "chips" will be golden, crunchy and lighter-than-air.*

Celery Root "Chips"

Vegetable oil, for deep-frying
1 small celery root, about 8 ounces, peeled, trimmed and sliced paper-thin

In a large heavy saucepan, heat the oil to 375 degrees F. Using a skimmer, fry the slices of celery root for 4 to 5 minutes, or until crisp and golden. Drain on paper towels and set aside.

Celery Root Mousse

1 large or 2 small celery roots, about
* 1 1/4 pounds total, peeled, trimmed*
* and cut into 2-inch chunks*

2 cups milk
1/4 cup unsalted butter
Salt and freshly ground white pepper

In a medium saucepan, combine the celery root with the milk (add water if necessary to be sure all the chunks are covered with liquid) and bring to a simmer. Cook for 25 to 30 minutes, or until tender, then put through the fine disk of a food mill or mash with a masher and return to the pan. Over low heat, stir in the butter and salt and pepper to taste. Set aside, covered.

Venison Stock

1/4 cup (2 ounces) unsalted butter
Bones and trimmings from the venison loin,
* chopped into 2-inch pieces*
5 medium shallots, coarsely chopped
1 medium carrot, coarsely chopped
1 tablespoon coarsely cracked black pepper

1 cup port
1 sprig fresh thyme
1 bay leaf
2 cloves garlic, unpeeled
1 quart red wine
1 1/2 quarts chicken stock (see page 136)

Preheat the oven to 400 degrees F. In a large ovenproof braising or roasting pan, heat half of the butter over medium-high heat. Add the bones and trimmings and sauté for 5 to 6 minutes, turning with kitchen tongs until nicely browned all over. Add the shallots, carrot, pepper and remaining butter, stir to mix thoroughly and roast in the oven for 15 to 20 minutes, stirring once or twice during the cooking

time, until dark brown and caramelized. Remove from the oven and pour off the fat. Return the pan to the stove top over medium heat and deglaze with the port, stirring and scraping the bottom and sides to release all the flavorful bits into the liquid. Add the thyme, bay leaf and garlic, and continue to cook until the liquid is reduced by half. Add the wine and stir to mix, then simmer, stirring occasionally, until the wine has evaporated almost completely, watching carefully that it doesn't go too far and burn. Add the stock, bring the liquid to a simmer, cover and cook for 1 hour. Strain the stock through a strainer lined with a double thickness of slightly dampened cheesecloth into a small saucepan, pressing down hard on the solids to extract all their flavor; discard the solids. Again, bring the stock to a simmer and reduce by about two-thirds, or until about 1 1/4 cups of liquid remains. Set aside, covered, until you are ready for the final assembly.

Venison

2 tablespoons unsalted butter
8 medallions of venison loin, about 2 1/2 ounces each and 1 1/2 to 2 inches thick
Salt and freshly ground white pepper

In a large sauté pan, heat the butter over medium-high heat until the foam has subsided and the butter is very hot. Add the medallions and cook for 1 to 2 minutes on each side, then reduce the heat, cover the pan and cook for 2 minutes more, until the outside is nice and brown and the inside is still pink. Season to taste with salt and pepper, then transfer to a plate and cover with aluminum foil while you finish the sauce.

Assembly

1/4 cup unsalted butter at room temperature, cut into 2 pieces
The venison medallions
2 ripe persimmons, peeled and halved (peel as you would a tomato, see page 139)

Bring the reduced venison stock back to a simmer. Remove from the heat and swirl in the butter, a piece at a time, stirring and swirling until it is completely absorbed. Gently reheat the celery root mousse. Using 2 teaspoons, make 12 quenelles of the mousse and place 3 in a fan shape on the bottom of each of 4 heated large dinner plates. Place 2 of the venison medallions on the top of the plate and garnish with a halved persimmon. Spoon some of the sauce over the top of the venison and around the plate and garnish with a few of the celery root chips.

SOMMELIER'S WINE CHOICE
Pahlmeyer Cabernet Sauvignon (Napa Valley)   Moraga Cabernet Sauvignon (Bel Air)

Roasted Fillet of Beef

IN HERB CRUST WITH FOREST MUSHROOM RAGOÛT

SERVES 4

Each slice of beef tenderloin will be about 2 1/2 inches thick, and when you slice into the center it should be a uniform pink with an outside that is nice and brown. Because the herb crust is difficult to make in small quantities, you will end up with about double the amount called for in this recipe. You can freeze the leftover crust and use it for topping any grilled or sautéed meat, game or poultry – but remember to remove it from the freezer and let it cool to room temperature before you use it.

Herb Crust

1 pound unsalted butter, at room temperature, cut into 8 pieces
8 slices fresh white bread, crusts removed, processed to fine bread crumbs in a food processor
    (about 3 cups bread crumbs)
2 tablespoons finely chopped chives
2 tablespoons finely chopped Italian (flat-leaf) parsley
5 cloves roasted garlic (see page 138)
Salt and freshly ground white pepper

In a food processor fitted with the metal blade, blend all the ingredients to a smooth and uniform paste. Scrape the mixture onto a long piece of plastic wrap and, using the plastic wrap, form the mixture into a cylinder 2 inches in diameter and about 11 inches long. Wrap well and refrigerate until needed.

Beef Fillets

The reserved herb crust
2 tablespoons unsalted butter
Four 5-ounce slices beef tenderloin, trimmed
Salt and freshly ground white pepper

Preheat the oven to 400 degrees F. Remove the herb crust from the refrigerator and unwrap. In an ovenproof sauté pan large enough to hold all the fillets, melt the butter over medium-high heat. Add the fillets and sauté for 2 to 3 minutes, or until browned on one side, then turn to the other side and put the pan in the hot oven to finish cooking for 3 to 4 minutes, or until just below medium rare. Season with salt and pepper. Slice four 1/2-inch-thick slices of the herb crust and place 1 slice of herb crust atop each fillet.

Mushroom Ragoût

1 cup (4 ounces) fresh morel mushrooms, with stems trimmed and halved; or dried morels,
    soaked for 20 minutes in very hot water and squeezed dry
1/3 cup unsalted butter, divided
2 medium shallots, finely chopped
1 cup chicken stock (see page 136)
4 cups (1 pound) assorted seasonal mushrooms, such as cèpes, oyster, chanterelles, black
    trumpet, shiitake or domestic, according to availability, brushed clean and quartered
Salt and freshly ground white pepper

Wash the morels in 2 or 3 changes of water in order to remove any dirt or small insects that may be lodged inside the caps. Dry them with paper towels. In a large sauté pan, melt 2 tablespoons of the butter over medium-low heat. Add the shallots and sweat for 3 to 4 minutes, or until translucent. Add the morels and cook slowly without browning for 2 to 3 minutes, or until they have given up their liquid. Add the stock and simmer, partially covered, until the morels are tender, about 15 minutes. Remove from the heat and allow to cool in their jus. In a medium sauté pan, heat the remaining 1/4 cup of the butter over medium heat and add the mixed seasonal mushrooms. Sauté for 4 to 5 minutes, stirring frequently, until cooked through. Drain the mushrooms briefly on paper towels and add to the morels and their jus. Season to taste with salt and pepper and set aside, covered, until you are ready to assemble the dish.

Assembly

1/2 cup red wine sauce (see page 138)
1/2 cup unsalted butter, at room temperature, cut into 4 equal pieces
1 medium shallot, finely chopped
1 tablespoon finely chopped chives

Preheat a broiler to high heat. In a small saucepan, bring the red wine sauce to a simmer and pour into a blender. Blend at high speed and add half the butter, a piece at a time, blending just until completely emulsified. Pour into a glass measuring cup and spoon off any foam that rises to the top. Gently reheat the mushroom ragoût and stir in the remaining butter, the shallot and chives. Place the beef fillets with their herb crust under the hot broiler and grill until the top is nicely browned. On each of 4 heated large dinner plates, mound some of the mushroom ragoût. Top with a crusted fillet and spoon some of the red wine sauce around the plate.

SOMMELIER'S WINE CHOICE
Duckhorn Merlot "Three Palms" (Napa Valley)
Château Latour Bordeaux (Pomerol)

7:30 p.m.

The waiters are carting in quantities of dirty dishes, and from this point on the ordinary kitchen racket of sizzling, chopping and "How long on the scallop roll?" competes with a formidable clatter of silverware being washed in stainless-steel sinks.

Over the racket is Jonny Fernow's voice. He's shouting, "Andy, I'm hurtin' here, I'm waitin'." A waiter has come in to deliver explicit instructions from a customer at table 9 who has ordered kidneys. **"That table's super-JBS,"** calls Joachim. "I want to taste everything."

"Yellowtail is running out," says Jonny. "We're switching to whitefish. Tell all the waiters." The last step in dishing up is often adding one of the colorful fried garnishes: onion threads, leek threads, *carrot threads* or slices. The waiters wipe the rims of the plates clean with towels before taking them out. Sometimes Joachim does this himself.

The waiter comes back to re-emphasize that table 9 wants its *kidneys* rare. "We have a kidney on board," calls the sous-chef. "So don't fire anything."

"What's the exact time now?" somebody wants to know. Two chefs call out that it's 7:46.

At 7:50 there's a lull on the line, due to the fact that there's only one seating for parties in private rooms and all of these have been seated. Joachim tells Jonny and the dinner pastry chef how to handle *fraise du bois*. "Don't wash them," he says. "We plate them with a vanilla sauce. By the way, the polenta for tomorrow – make it very thick, so we can do quenelles. It'll look nice." Then things pick up again. Dishes clatter, waiters pop in and out, orders are torn off the printer and called.

"How much time?" Jonny demands from the range.

"Fourteen minutes."

"Where's the onion salad? I need it."

"I'm still waiting on that *cannelloni*."

"One minute, chef, one."

"Nine minutes to go," calls Joachim. "We go with 2 first, then 4 salmon, 7 lamb, 5 and 5 and 7 and 3."

While the line chefs are leaping around in a nervous ballet, the chef at the pastry station is calmly arranging mousses and tarts just so, stirring traceries of *raspberry sauce* into pools of crème anglaise with a toothpick, adjusting garnishes of praline, tapping a dusting of *cocoa* onto the rims of plates.

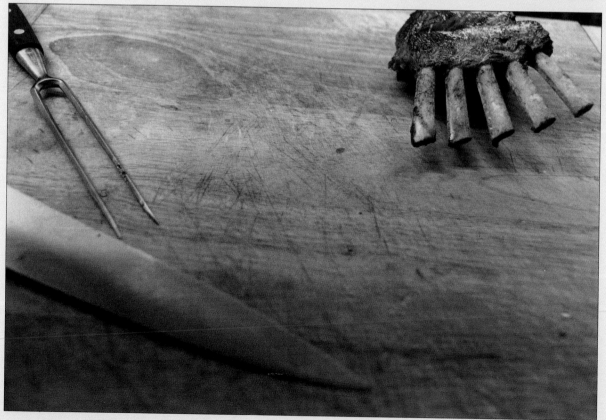

LATER SATURDAY NIGHT, KITCHEN

8:15 p.m.

A back waiter walks too close to the swinging kitchen door, it opens in his face, and he drops a coffee tray with a hellish noise. Everybody jumps. Joachim lectures him on the right way to walk around a swinging door.

Now there's an emergency: Some dishes are getting done too soon. "Don't go on that fish; we need the appetizers first."

"Andrea, hold the tuna!"

A waiter sticks his head in the door. "First ones all medium-rare at that table."

"Twenty-three is out."

"Fire 1," calls Joachim. "That's the last big table we fire before the party." A chef mumbles something. "Hey," Joachim snaps. "How do I hear you?"

A waiter brings a steak back and asks for it to be held for a minute to confirm an order. "Laurent!" Joachim shouts. "Is the party cleared? Check it."

Joachim pores through the order slips. "One thing I need before we go out is the duck liver."

"Get him the duck liver," says Jonny.

"Now we go with the party," says Joachim. "Entrées: eight lobsters, six veal, four lamb." He notices that the chef is putting four *lamb chops* on each plate instead of three. They all have to be rearranged, keeping the rares and medium-rares separate.

"Tomato raviolli, how long?"

"Right now."

"Right behind with the lamb."

"Fire me table 5."

"Yes, sir."

"And table 23."

"Yes, sir."

"Is that lamb medium-rare? Look at the order, they all want it medium-rare at that table. And I don't want anything sent back."

"How's the ravioli?"

"I've got too much ravioli."

"Mushroom ravioli for table 9."

"Up in two minutes."

"Make sure the *kidneys* are rare," injects a waiter. "The guy is the biggest pain on earth."

"I need one *green asparagus*, no onion," calls another.

"Yow! No onion?" Jonny professes to be shocked.

"I need a JBS dessert pickup, please."

At last the orders stop coming in.

"
How do I come up with a new dish?
I open the fridge. Or I sit home reading books.
Or I get a new kitchen machine."
"

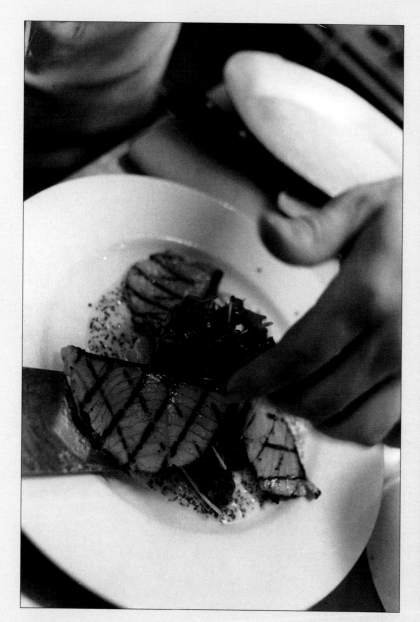

Roasted Duck
WITH BRAISED FIGS IN PORT WINE SAUCE

SERVES 4

*I prefer to use purple figs, such as California's Mission figs, for this beautiful dish. You could serve the legs and thighs of the duck (which will be crisp and golden)
as the next course on a salad of frisée, gently fried bacon lardons, chives and walnut vinaigrette (see page 54).*

Duck and Jus

2 ducks, about 3 pounds each
Salt and freshly ground white pepper
1/4 cup unsalted butter
2 medium carrots, finely chopped
6 medium shallots, coarsely chopped
1 whole head of garlic, halved
1 cup port
2 sprigs fresh thyme
2 cups chicken stock (see page 136)

Preheat the oven to 400 degrees F. Truss the ducks and season with salt and pepper.

In a large ovenproof sauté pan with high sides, heat the butter over medium-high heat. When the foam has subsided and the butter is very hot, sauté the ducks, one at a time if necessary, breast side down, using kitchen tongs to steady them, for 12 to 15 minutes, or until the fat has been rendered away and the skin is golden. Turn the ducks breast side up, transfer the pan to the hot oven and roast, basting every 4 to 5 minutes with the fat from the pan, for 12 to 15 minutes, or until the breasts are pink. Remove to a work surface and pour off and discard all but 1/4 cup of the fat from the pan.

Make a shallow cut along either side of the breastbone and remove each breast from the rib cage, cutting through the wing joint close to the body and leaving the first joint of the wing attached, but removing the wing tip. Set aside in a roasting pan covered with aluminum foil until you are ready to assemble the dish.

Remove the legs and thighs and cut the carcasses in half, then return to the pan with the carrots, shallots and garlic and roast in the oven for an additional 15 to 20 minutes, stirring occasionally, or until browned and almost caramelized. Set the legs and thighs aside for another use (see headnote).

Tilt the pan and, pushing the solids aside, spoon off and discard the remaining fat from the pan. On the top of the stove, add the port and thyme to the pan and deglaze, stirring and scraping the bottom and sides to release all the flavorful bits into the liquid. Over medium-high heat, reduce until the port has evaporated almost completely away, stirring occasionally and watching to be sure it does not go too far and burn. Add the stock and reduce the heat to medium. Reduce the mixture by about half, so that a scant 1 cup liquid remains. Strain the stock through a sieve lined with a double thickness of slightly dampened cheesecloth into a small saucepan, pressing down hard on the solids to extract all their flavor. Discard the solids and set the pan aside, covered, until you are ready to finish the dish.

Figs and Spinach

6 medium purple figs
1 cup port
2 tablespoons unsalted butter
2 tablespoons finely chopped shallots
1/2 pound (8 cups) spinach, stems removed

Preheat the oven to 400 degrees F. In a small ovenproof sauté pan, combine the figs and the port (the port should come a third of the way up the figs). Bring to a simmer over medium heat, then transfer the pan to the hot oven and braise, basting every 2 to 3 minutes, for 6 to 8 minutes, or until the figs are tender and juicy but not mushy. Cut them into quarters and set aside, in the pan. In a medium sauté pan, melt the butter over medium heat and add the shallots. Sauté for 3 to 4 minutes, or until softened. Add the spinach and toss together to coat, just until wilted.

Assembly

2 tablespoons unsalted butter
Salt and freshly ground white pepper

Reheat the duck breasts in a low oven, if necessary. Bring the duck jus back to a simmer over medium heat and swirl in the butter, stirring until it is just absorbed. Immediately remove the pan from the heat and add salt and pepper to taste. With a slotted spoon, remove the figs from their jus and mound a quarter of them on each of 4 heated large dinner plates. Mound some of the spinach on the other side of the plate. Slice the duck breasts into 1/2-inch-thick slices and fan out one breast over the spinach on each plate. Spoon some of both the duck and the fig jus over the top.

SOMMELIER'S WINE CHOICE
Robert Mondavi Cabernet Sauvignon "Reserve" (Napa Valley)
Staglin Cabernet Sauvignon (Napa Valley)

Roasted Partridge

WITH CABBAGE, PEARL ONIONS, APPLE-SMOKED BACON AND FRIED PARSNIPS

SERVES 4

When I cook game, I like to combine it with distinctly flavored, earthy ingredients that can stand up to the meat's own strong flavors.

POULTRY AND GAME BIRD MAIN COURSES

Partridge and Sauce

4 partridges, about 14 ounces each,
    with legs and feet attached
Salt and freshly ground white pepper
1/2 cup unsalted butter

1 medium carrot, sliced thick
4 medium shallots, sliced thick
1/2 cup dry white wine
2 cups chicken stock (see page 136)

Preheat the oven to 400 degrees F. Truss and season the partridges with salt and pepper.

In a large ovenproof sauté pan, heat the butter over medium-high heat. When the butter is very hot and the foam has subsided, sear the birds on both sides of the breast for 1 to 2 minutes. Turn the birds breast side up and place the pan in the hot oven to finish cooking, basting the breasts with the pan drippings every 2 minutes, for about 8 minutes more, or until the breasts are pink.

Set the birds on a cutting board and make a shallow cut down either side of the breastbone. Remove the boneless breasts from the rib cage with their wing joints, legs and thighs and set them aside on an ovenproof plate, covered with aluminum foil. Return the carcasses to the pan and add the carrot and shallots. Toss to mix and return the pan to the hot oven for about 10 minutes, until the legs are cooked all the way through.

Remove the legs and reserve them with the breasts. Continue roasting the carcasses and vegetables, stirring occasionally, for 10 to 15 minutes, or until caramelized, and then pour off and discard the excess fat. Return the pan to the stove top over medium heat and deglaze with the wine, stirring and scraping the bottom and sides to release all the flavorful bits into the liquid. Add the stock and reduce the mixture by two-thirds, until a little over 1 cup of liquid remains. Strain through a strainer lined with a double thickness of slightly dampened cheesecloth into a small saucepan, pressing down hard on the solids to extract all their flavor; discard the solids. Bring the sauce to a simmer again and reduce to just over 1/2 cup liquid. Set aside, covered.

Fried Parsnips Strips

1/4 pound parsnips (about 2 small), peeled
Vegetable oil for deep-frying

With a vegetable peeler, cut the parsnips into long strips. In a large heavy saucepan, heat the oil to 375 degrees F and, using a skimmer, deep-fry the parsnip strips for 30 to 60 seconds, or until crisp and brown. Drain on paper towels and, when the strips are cool enough to handle but still quite warm, press them into 4 loose balls and set aside.

Cabbage, Pearl Onion and Bacon Garniture

3 tablespoons unsalted butter at room temperature, cut into 3 pieces
16 pearl onions, peeled
Salt and freshly ground white pepper
1/2 teaspoon sugar
1/4 cup chicken stock
4 ounces apple-smoked bacon, cut into fine julienne strips
10 ounces small inner leaves of white cabbage, blanched for 2 minutes in boiling water, drained
    and torn into bite-sized pieces
Salt and freshly ground white pepper

In a small saucepan, heat 1 tablespoon of the butter over medium-high heat and add the pearl onions, salt and pepper to taste and sugar. Sauté for 5 to 6 minutes, stirring frequently, or until caramelized. Add the stock and simmer the onions until they are tender, about 6 minutes. Remove from the heat and set aside. Heat another small saucepan over medium-low heat. Add the bacon and cook gently so that all the fat renders out but the bacon does not brown. Add the onions with their jus and the cabbage and stir until the mixture is very hot. Simmer, stirring, for 2 to 3 minutes, or until the liquid is slightly reduced. Add the remaining 2 tablespoons of butter and stir constantly until the garniture is bound with a creamy emulsification, then remove from the heat. Season to taste with salt and pepper and set aside.

Assembly

2 ounces "A" grade duck liver or chicken liver, cut into 1/4-inch cubes, (optional)
1 tablespoon finely chopped flat-leaf (Italian) parsley

Preheat the oven to 400 degrees F and reheat the partridge parts for 1 to 2 minutes, or until warmed through. Add the cubed duck liver to the garniture and reheat over high heat for 20 to 30 seconds, until just heated through and the liver begins to "melt." Divide the mixture among 4 heated large dinner plates, mounding it in the center, and place 2 breast and wing pieces on top of the garniture. Place the reserved legs on either side of the breast so that the feet stick up into the air and meet in the middle. Reheat the sauce just to a simmer, remove from the heat and stir in the parsley, then spoon it over the partridge and its garniture. Top each with a ball of deep-fried parsnip strips.

SOMMELIER'S WINE CHOICE
Spottswoode Cabernet Sauvignon (Napa Valley)
Heitz Cellars Cabernet Sauvignon "Martha's Vineyard" (Napa Valley)

Roasted Farm Chicken Breast

WITH CARROT ROUNDS AND FRESH THYME LEMON SAUCE

SERVES 4

At its heart this is a simple dish; the flavors of lemon, thyme, carrots and chicken just seem to be made for one another.
If you are friendly with your butcher, ask him to perform the jointing of the chicken.

Broth

2 farm-raised or free-range chickens, about 3 pounds each
1 tablespoon unsalted butter
2 ribs celery, coarsely chopped
1/2 medium onion, coarsely chopped
1 medium carrot, coarsely chopped
1/2 clove garlic, peeled
1/2 cup white wine
3 cups chicken stock (see page 136)
1 cup water
2 sprigs fresh thyme

Keeping the skin on, remove the breasts and the first wing joint in one piece from each of the chickens, halve the breasts into 4 single breasts and set aside, covered and refrigerated. Remove the legs and thighs and reserve for another use. Using a heavy cleaver or poultry shears, chop the carcasses into 2-inch pieces.

In a large saucepan, heat the butter over medium heat until it just turns brown. Add the carcass pieces and roast, stirring occasionally, for 8 to 10 minutes, or until nicely browned. Pour off and discard the excess fat from the pan and add the celery, onion, carrot and garlic. Cook for an additional 5 minutes, or until the vegetables are softened. Add the wine, reduce until almost dry, then add the stock, water and thyme and bring to a simmer. Cook the broth over low heat, uncovered, for 45 minutes, occasionally skimming any fats and impurities from the top with a large flat spoon. Strain through a strainer lined with a double thickness of slightly dampened cheesecloth into a small saucepan, pressing down on the solids to extract all of their flavor. Discard the solids. You should have about 2 1/2 cups of broth.

Carrot Rounds

1 tablespoon unsalted butter
3 medium shallots, finely chopped
3/4 pound large carrots, sliced into 1/8-inch rounds (about 2 1/2 cups, sliced)
1 cup of the reserved chicken broth
Salt and freshly ground white pepper

In a medium saucepan, melt the butter over medium heat. Add the shallots and sauté, stirring occasionally, for 3 to 4 minutes, or until just softened. Add the carrot rounds, broth and salt and pepper to taste and bring to a boil. Reduce the heat so that the broth is just simmering and cook, covered, for about 10 to 12 minutes, or until the carrots are al dente. Set aside, and when cool, refrigerate, if desired.

Thyme Lemon Butter

1/4 cup unsalted butter, at room temperature
1 teaspoon finely chopped lemon zest
Juice of 1 lemon
1 teaspoon finely chopped fresh thyme or 1/2 teaspoon dried
Salt and freshly ground white pepper

In a small bowl, combine the butter with the lemon zest, lemon juice, thyme and salt and pepper to taste. Mix together well with a fork and set aside.

Carrot Threads

4 large carrots (about 3/4 pound)
1 quart vegetable oil

Using a mandoline or a vegetable peeler, cut the carrots into long sheets and then cut the sheets into long 1/8-inch-thick threads. You should have about 4 cups of loosely packed carrot threads.

In a large heavy pan, heat the oil to 350 degrees F. Cook the carrots in 2 batches, frying each batch for 1 to 1 1/2 minutes, or until crisp. Remove to a baking tin lined with paper towels to drain and, when cool enough to handle but still quite warm, form the threads into 4 loose balls. *(continued on next page)*

Chicken

The reserved chicken breasts
Salt and freshly ground white pepper
2 tablespoons unsalted butter
1 1/2 cups of the reserved chicken broth

Preheat the oven to 400 degrees F. Season the chicken breasts with salt and pepper. In a large ovenproof sauté pan heat 1 tablespoon of the butter over medium-high heat. When the foam has subsided and the butter is very hot, add the chicken breasts, skin side down, and cook for about 1 minute. Turn the breasts to the other side, place the pan in the hot oven and cook for 20 to 25 minutes, or until the chicken is done all the way through and no trace of pink remains. Remove the breasts to an ovenproof plate and cover with aluminum foil.

Add the chicken broth to the pan and, over medium-high heat, reduce by half, or down to thick coating consistency. Add the remaining tablespoon of butter to the chicken jus in the pan and stir and swirl just until absorbed. Set aside.

Assembly

The reserved carrot rounds
The reserved thyme lemon butter
4 tablespoons finely chopped Italian (flat-leaf) parsley
The reserved deep-fried carrot balls
The reserved chicken breasts and jus

Allow the carrot rounds to come to room temperature and preheat the oven to 350 degrees F.

With a slotted spoon, remove the carrots from their cooking liquid to another small saucepan. Stir the thyme lemon butter into the carrots and warm the mixture gently over low heat. Stir in the chopped parsley and remove from the heat. Place the deep-fried carrot balls and the chicken breasts in the hot oven for 2 minutes just to warm through.

Spoon some of the warm carrot rounds with their jus onto each of 4 heated large dinner plates, mounding them in the center. Slice each chicken breast into 3 thick slices and arrange them over the carrot rounds, with the wing joint facing upward. Spoon a little of the chicken jus over the top and decorate each serving with a deep-fried carrot ball.

SOMMELIER'S WINE CHOICE
Ponsot Morey-Saint-Denis (Red Burgundy, Côte de Nuits)
Courcel Pommard "Epenots" (Red Burgundy, Côte de Beaune)

Pheasant
WITH CARAMELIZED SALSIFY AND BANYULS SAUCE

SERVES 4

Each year when the game season begins, Patina features several game dishes that never fail to draw out the game lovers who have waited patiently all summer. This is one of our best. Banyuls is a fortified sweet and fruity red wine from Languedoc-Roussillon, in southwest France. It has a distinctive flavor, called "rancio," that comes from exposing the barrels to direct sunlight, sometimes for as long as two years. In a pinch you could substitute port, but the flavor will not be the same.

Pheasant and Sauce

2 whole pheasants, about 1 3/4 pounds each
Salt and freshly ground white pepper
1/3 cup unsalted butter
1 medium carrot, coarsely chopped
5 medium shallots, coarsely chopped
1 teaspoon coarsely cracked black pepper
1 quart dry red wine
2 sprigs fresh thyme
1 bay leaf
2 cups chicken stock (see page 136)
1/4 cup (2 ounces) Banyuls wine or port

Preheat the oven to 400 degrees F. Truss and then season the pheasants with salt and pepper.

In a large ovenproof sauté pan with high sides, heat the butter over medium-high heat. When the foam has subsided and the butter is very hot, sauté each pheasant in turn, breast side down, using kitchen tongs to steady them, for 3 to 4 minutes, or until just golden. Turn the birds breast side up, transfer the pan to the hot oven and roast, basting every 2 minutes with the butter from the pan, for 20 minutes or until the breasts are rosy (they will be gently reheated later). Remove to a work surface.

Make a shallow cut along either side of the breastbone and remove each breast from the rib cage, cutting through the wing joint close to the body and leaving the wing attached. Set the breasts aside in a roasting pan, covered with aluminum foil, until you are ready to assemble the dish.

Remove the legs and thighs and cut the carcasses into 2-inch pieces, then return all of them to the pan with the carrot, shallots and pepper and roast in the oven for an additional 15 to 20 minutes, stirring occasionally, until browned and almost caramelized. Tilt the pan and, pushing the solids aside, spoon off and discard the accumulated fat. On top of the stove, add the wine to the pan and deglaze, stirring and scraping the bottom and sides to release all the flavorful bits into the liquid. Add the thyme and bay leaf and, over medium-high heat, reduce until the wine has evaporated almost completely, stirring occasionally and watching to be sure it doesn't go too far and burn. Add the stock and reduce the heat to medium. Simmer, partially covered, for 40 minutes. Strain the stock through a sieve lined with a double thickness of slightly dampened cheesecloth into a small saucepan, pressing down hard on the solids to extract all their flavor. You should have about 1 cup of stock.

Set the legs and thighs aside in the roasting pan with the breasts, and discard the carcass pieces and vegetables. Add the Banyuls wine to the stock and continue to reduce over medium-high heat until a scant 1 cup of liquid remains. Set aside.

Salsify

1 pound fresh salsify root, peeled and cut on the diagonal into 2-inch lengths
2 cups milk

In a medium saucepan, combine the salsify and milk and bring to a simmer over medium heat. Cook for 6 to 8 minutes, or until al dente, then drain and set aside. Reserve the milk for vegetable soup, if desired.

Assembly

1/2 cup unsalted butter
Salt and freshly ground white pepper
1 teaspoon finely chopped Italian (flat-leaf) parsley

Preheat the oven to 350 degrees F. In a medium sauté pan, melt 2 tablespoons of the butter over medium-high heat. Add the salsify and salt and pepper to taste and cook, stirring frequently, for 2 to 3 minutes, or until the salsify is golden. Remove from the heat and stir in the parsley. Bring the sauce back to a simmer, remove from the heat and swirl in the remaining 2 tablespoons of butter, stirring and swirling until the butter is completely absorbed and the sauce is glossy.

To serve, reheat the pheasant breasts, legs and thighs in the hot oven for 2 to 3 minutes, or until warmed through. Slice the breasts and fan out 1 breast at the top of each of 4 heated large dinner plates. Arrange 1 leg and thigh opposite the breast, spoon a generous amount of sauce over the meat and mound some of the salsify on the side.

SOMMELIER'S WINE CHOICE
Dunn Cabernet Sauvignon "Howell Mountain" (Napa Valley)
Château Lynch-Bages Bordeaux (Pauillac)

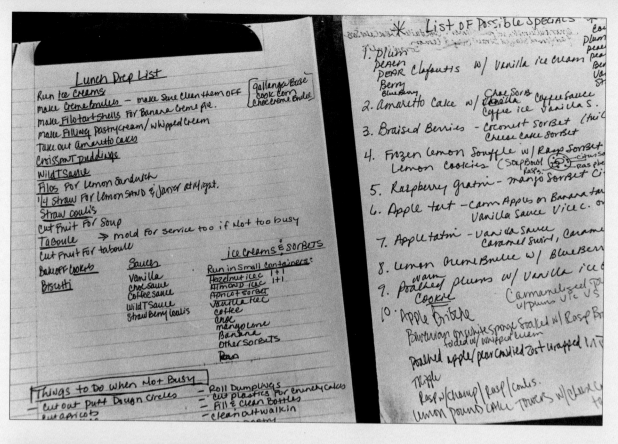

Lunch Prep List

- Run Ice creams
- make Creme brûlées — make sure clean them OFF
- make Filo tart shells For Banana Creme pie.
- make Filling pastry cream / whipped cream
- Take out Amaretto cakes
- Croissant Puddings
- WildT Sauce
- Filos For Lemon Sandwich
- 1/4 Straw For Lemon SAND & Janer at Night.
- Straw coulis
- Cut Fruit For Soup
- Taboule → mold For service too if Not too busy
- Cut Fruit For taboulé
- Bake off cookies
- Biscotti

(top right box)
Gallanga Base
cook corn
choc crème brulée

Sauces
- Vanilla
- Choc sauce
- Coffee sauce
- WildT Sauce
- Strawberry Coulis

Ice creams & Sorbets

Run in Small Containers:
- Hazelnut ice c   1+1
- Almond icec   1+1
- Apricot sorbet
- Vanilla ice c
- coffee
- choc
- mango lime
- banana
- Other Sorbets
- Pear

Things to do when Not Busy
- Cut out puff Dough Circles
- cut apricots
- Roll Dumplings
- cut plastics for crunchy cakes
- Fill & clean Bottles
- clean out walk in
- pastry

---

1. Plum / Peach / PEAR / Berry / Blueberry Clafoutis w/ Vanilla ice cream
2. Amaretto cake w/ Choc Sorb & coffee sauce / Vanilla / coffee ice / Vanilla S.
3. Braised Berries – Coconut Sorbet (thick) Cheese cake Sorbet
4. Frozen Lemon Souffle w/ Rasp Sorbet Lemon Cookies (Soap Bowl) citrus so / Raspberry Rasp.
5. Raspberry gratin – mango sorbet Ci
6. Apple tart – carm Apples on Banana tar Vanilla sauce V ice c. or
7. Apple tatin – Vanilla sauce, caramel Caramel swirl, Carame
8. Lemon creme Brulee w/ BlueBerry
9. warm Poached plums w/ Vanilla ice c Cookie Caramelized / w/ plums V ic c V S
10. Apple Brioche
    Bavarian on white sponge Soaked w/ Rasp B folded w/ whipped cream
    Poached apple/pear candied zest wrapped in T
    Triffle
    Rasp w/ champ / Rasp / coulis.
    Lemon Pound cake Towers w/ Cher c

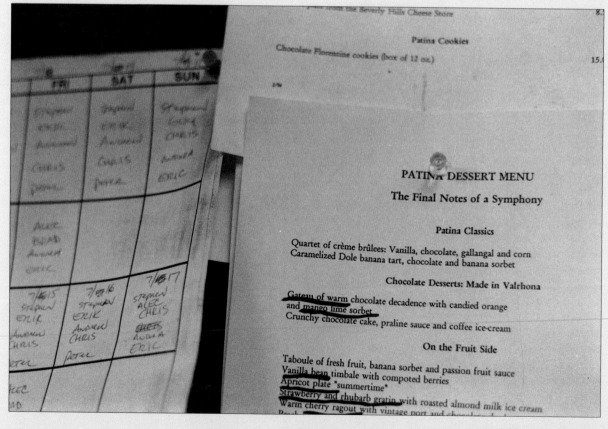

(calendar)

FRI	SAT	SUN
...	...	...
7/15	7/16	7/17
STEPHEN ERIK ANDREW CHRIS	STEPHEN ERIK ANDREW CHRIS	STEPHEN ALEX CHRIS CHRIS ANDREW ERIK

(printed menu, top)

from the Beverly Hills Cheese Store   8.

Patina Cookies

Chocolate Florentine cookies (box of 12 oz.)   15.

PATINA DESSERT MENU

The Final Notes of a Symphony

Patina Classics

Quartet of crème brûlées: Vanilla, chocolate, gallangal and corn
Caramelized Dole banana tart, chocolate and banana sorbet

Chocolate Desserts: Made in Valrhona

Gateau of warm chocolate decadence with candied orange and mango lime sorbet
Crunchy chocolate cake, praline sauce and coffee ice-cream

On the Fruit Side

Taboule of fresh fruit, banana sorbet and passion fruit sauce
Vanilla bean timbale with compoted berries
Apricot plate "summertime"
Strawberry and rhubarb gratin with roasted almond milk ice cream
Warm cherry ragout with vintage port and chocolate
Peach

PASTRY KITCHEN

8:00 a.m.

Like the prep kitchen that adjoins it, the pastry kitchen (as distinguished from the pastry *station* down in the kitchen, where desserts are dished up) is a world of its own. Its schedule is only loosely related to the perennial emergency downstairs.

The pastry day begins at 8:00 a.m., when the morning pastry chef starts baking off tart crusts and *brioche* in an oven that's located next door in the prep kitchen. The oven is outside the pastry kitchen because a lot of *chocolate confections* wouldn't last more than few moments in the same room with an oven.

9:00 a.m. Head pastry chef Victor Cordes arrives to consult with

a client about a wedding cake order. The morning chef starts making brioche dough for tomorrow's baking, makes various cookies and *biscotti*, poaches apricots and peaches and then bakes them in foil tartlet tins. Since the tart crusts are already baked, the line pastry chef working downstairs during a meal will be able to do the impossible – instantly whip up a warm apple tart to order by inverting the cooked fruit onto a crust and caramelizing it with a propane blowtorch.

In the case of the banana tarts, **caramelizing with the blowtorch** is actually all it takes to cook the banana slices. The only dessert that needs actual oven time at the last minute is the warm *chocolate gateau*, five minutes' warm-up.

2:00 p.m. The dinner pastry chef joins the morning chef and head chef

Cordes, who's been in and out all morning. Carefully at a distance from the dessert pastries, he bakes a tray of garlic tarts – an appetizer whimsy consisting of flower-shaped wisps of *phyllo* studded with bits of garlic.

In the corner, by the single, tiny sink, are a floor-model mixer and a *sorbet* maker with a sharp brass scraper. The kitchen has three working surfaces: marble for *chocolate*, wood for dough, stainless steel for other jobs. The latter also has a burner and a propane torch. On an island in the middle of the room are a scale, flats of *eggs*, a black box of pastry chef's tools and a stockpot containing sugar syrup for the sorbets. Next to it is the recipe, written on a paper towel: Syrup 13c sugar 1 kilo H_2O.

4:00 p.m. The dinner pastry chef pipes raspberry purée onto little pecan

cookies. Then he whips a *sabayon sauce* of eggs, sugar and champagne. Chunks of rhubarb are being poached in zip-lock bags so that they don't get mushy.

The baked pastry elements, such as tart shells, are stored on trays; the sauces, mousses and creams, together with moist desserts such as crème brûlées and Bavarians, go into the refrigerator; the ice creams and sorbets into the freezer.

5:20 p.m. Victor picks up the phone. "Would you bring a small plate of

food upstairs? I can't get away." In a few minutes a plate of *bow-tie pasta*, sautéed beef and salad appears. The "clock" on the wall is actually Victor's wristwatch, pinned up. There's no percentage wearing a watch when you're working with flour and chocolate.

You get a feel for whether a dish is coming out right, even without tasting it. It's like a parent-child relationship. You know if your kid doesn't look well.

PASTRY KITCHEN

5:30 p.m.

The lunch and dinner pastry chefs are having pasta for dinner. "Really a lot of garlic in this pasta," says one. A waiter comes upstairs to get a few loaves of brioche.

Jonny Fernow shows up. "The party of 12 really wants some cookies for tonight," he says. The morning chef hauls down a tray of *chocolate biscotti.*

6:00 p.m.
The morning pastry chef goes home. Victor starts working on a chocolate mousse birthday cake with *raspberry* filling. He frosts it with dark chocolate, and in a few lightning movements, decorates the top with a complex tracery of white *chocolate.* Then he starts tonight's special dessert: disks of vanilla génoise, looking curiously like hamburger buns, will be covered with lemon curd and raspberries and surrounded by a ribbon of white and dark chocolate.

The *chocolate ribbon* must be handled at temperatures below 80 degrees Fahrenheit, because it involves tempering the chocolate, a matter of mixing cooled chocolate with melted chocolate and working the mixture at decreasing temperatures until it reaches a consistency that will solidify smoothly. Under the long marble counter is a **freezing system** that creates a range of temperatures along its length.

Victor works *white chocolate* to the consistency he wants, spreads it on a thin strip of parchment paper, waits a moment, then scrapes it with a metal tool, removing a layer from the top. When the white chocolate cools, he covers it with a layer of *dark chocolate,* creating a white and dark stripe. Just before it stiffens, he wraps the ribbon around the disk of cake and puts it in the cold room to harden.

At 7:30 p.m. the dinner line chef goes downstairs. Victor works alone for the rest of the evening, making tray after tray of chocolate decorations and putting them in the freezer.

Quartet of Crème Brûlées:
CORN, VANILLA, GALANGA AND CHOCOLATE

SERVES 4

This is one of our most popular desserts. Galanga is a cousin of ginger; the fresh root is available only at Thai markets, so if you can't find it, substitute fresh ginger. You will need a total of 16 tiny 2-ounce ramekins for this recipe. It can easily be prepared the day before up to the finishing stage, and indeed the flavor of the crèmes will improve.

DESSERTS

Custard Base for Corn, Vanilla and Galanga

2 1/2 cups heavy cream
1 vanilla bean, halved lengthwise and seeds scraped out and reserved
8 large egg yolks
1/2 cup plus 1 tablespoon granulated sugar
1 teaspoon grated galanga root, if available, or substitute grated fresh ginger
1/4 cup corn kernels, cooked for 1 minute in 1/4 cup boiling water with 2 tablespoons sugar and drained

In a medium saucepan, bring the cream to a boil with the vanilla pod and seeds. Remove from the heat and allow to infuse for 10 to 15 minutes. Strain out the vanilla pod. In a large mixing bowl, whisk the egg yolks and the sugar together until well blended. Slowly add the warm cream, whisking to blend well. Divide the custard mixture into 3 equal portions. In a large glass measuring cup, combine a third of the mixture with the grated galanga or ginger and allow to infuse for at least 1 hour.

Assemble 12 ramekins on the work surface. In the bottom of 4 ramekins, spoon a little of the cooked corn, then pour in plain custard mixture to reach almost to the top. Pour plain custard mixture almost to the top of 4 more ramekins. Using a strainer, strain the galanga-infused mixture into the remaining ramekins. Cover the first 3 types of custard with a tea towel while you make the chocolate custard.

Chocolate Custard

1 1/4 cups heavy cream
1/4 cup milk
1/4 vanilla bean, halved lengthwise and seeds scraped out and reserved
2 large egg yolks
1/4 cup granulated sugar
2 ounces bittersweet baking chocolate, broken into small pieces, melted

In a medium saucepan, bring the cream and milk to a boil with the vanilla pod and seeds. Remove from the heat and allow to infuse for 10 to 15 minutes. Strain out the pod. In a medium mixing bowl, whisk the egg yolks and sugar together until well blended, thickened and pale. Slowly add the warm cream to the yolk mixture, whisking to blend completely. Pour in the melted chocolate and blend well. Pour the chocolate mixture into the last 4 ramekins.

Cooking the Custards

Preheat the oven to 325 degrees F. Place all of the ramekins in the bottom of a large roasting pan and carefully pour in boiling water to come about halfway up their sides. Cover the pan tightly with aluminum foil and cook in the hot oven for 25 to 30 minutes. Cooking time will depend on the thickening power of the egg yolks, and you should check the custards frequently toward the end of the cooking time and remove them from the oven when the very center of each custard is just jiggly. Cool to room temperature and refrigerate for at least 1 hour or up to 24 hours.

Assembly

The prepared ramekins, very cold
1/2 cup raw sugar, firmly packed

Preheat a broiler to high heat. Using a sieve to be sure you get even coverage, sprinkle the sugar evenly over the tops of all of the ramekins. Place the ramekins, several at a time so that they are easier to manage, under the hot broiler just until the sugar has melted and caramelized to a deep golden brown. Watch carefully and turn them to be sure the tops caramelize evenly and do not burn. This is a tricky operation and you may get uneven results the first time, but if you like crème brûlée, I suggest you invest in a hand-held butane torch, which makes the caramelizing process a breeze. Repeat with the remaining custards and refrigerate them again until 15 minutes before you are ready to serve. To serve, on each of 4 dessert plates, fold a small cloth napkin and arrange 1 of each of the different crème brûlées on the plate.

Strawberry Rhubarb Pie
WITH STRAWBERRY SORBET

SERVES 6

My interpretation of an American classic, with a slightly different twist.

Strawberry Sorbet

2 cups water

2/3 cup granulated sugar

2 cups puréed fresh strawberries

1 large egg white, beaten to a light foam

1 tablespoon lemon juice

Make a simple syrup by dissolving the sugar in the water in a small saucepan and bringing it just to a boil over medium heat. Remove from the heat, cool and refrigerate until chilled. Combine with the strawberry purée, egg white and lemon juice and whisk to mix thoroughly. Freeze in an ice-cream maker according to the manufacturer's instructions.

Sugar Dough

3 1/2 cups all-purpose flour

1/2 cup granulated sugar

1/4 teaspoon baking powder

1 cup (8 ounces) cold unsalted butter, cut into 1/2-inch pieces

1 large egg, lightly beaten

1 to 2 tablespoons ice water, as needed

In a food processor fitted with the metal blade, combine the flour, sugar and baking powder and pulse until mixed. Add the butter and pulse 3 or 4 times until the mixture resembles coarse bread crumbs. Do not overprocess. Remove the lid and sprinkle over the egg and 1 tablespoon of the ice water. Process until the mixture forms a ball on the central column. If this does not happen within 10 to 15 seconds, you may need to add another tablespoon of water (this depends on the dryness of the flour). Turn the dough out onto plastic wrap, bring together into a ball and refrigerate for 1 to 2 hours to make it easier to roll out.

Almond Cream

1/3 cup plus 1 tablespoon blanched slivered almonds

1/2 cup plus 2 teaspoons confectioners' sugar

1/2 cup unsalted butter, softened

1/2 cup granulated sugar

2 large eggs, lightly beaten

In a food processor fitted with the metal blade, process the almonds and the sugar for 20 to 30 seconds, or until powdery. (When you rub the powder between your fingers there should be almost no trace of grit.) In the bowl of an electric mixer or with a wooden spoon, cream the butter and sugar together until light and pale. Stir in the eggs, 1 at a time, making sure the first egg is blended in before adding the next. Blend in the almond powder and refrigerate, covered, until needed.

Filling and Assembly

1/3 cup unsalted butter

1/4 cup granulated sugar

1 tablespoon cornstarch

1 pound rhubarb, cut into 1-inch cubes

1 pint strawberries, stems removed and cut into quarters

1 large egg, lightly beaten

1 tablespoon raw sugar

The reserved strawberry sorbet

4 sprigs fresh mint

Preheat the oven to 350 degrees F and remove the sugar dough from the refrigerator.

Roll out the dough on a lightly floured surface to a thickness of 1/8 inch and use it to line six 5-inch tart shells. Reserve the dough trimmings, rolled into a ball, wrapped and refrigerated. Refrigerate the tart shells for 20 minutes, then prick the bottoms of the shells and spread a layer of almond cream about 1/4 inch thick in the bottom of each shell. Bake in the oven for 12 to 15 minutes, or until the filling is slightly golden and firm. Leave the oven on if you plan to finish the pies right away.

In a small saucepan, combine the butter, sugar and cornstarch over medium-high heat and add the rhubarb. Simmer, stirring occasionally, for 6 to 8 minutes, or until tender, testing as you cook because rhubarb can overcook very easily. Remove from the heat, stir in the quartered strawberries and let stand for 2 minutes; drain thoroughly in a strainer for 10 minutes. Fill the pie shells with the fruit mixture.

If the oven is not still on, bring it back up to 350 degrees F. On a lightly floured work surface, roll out the remaining sugar dough to a 1/8-inch thickness and cut as many 1/2-inch strips of dough as possible. Lay the pastry strips across the pies in a lattice pattern, brush them with the beaten egg and sprinkle evenly with the raw sugar. Return to the oven and bake for a further 15 to 20 minutes, or until the pastry is golden. Serve warm with a scoop of the sorbet on the side, garnished with a sprig of mint.

SOMMELIER'S WINE CHOICE

Chateau Coutet Sauternes (Bordeaux) Domaine Baumard Quarts-de-Chaume (Loire)

Warm Chocolate Soufflés

WITH TANGERINE SORBET AND CITRUS SAUCE

SERVES 6

A wild contrast of flavors, textures and temperatures.
These soufflés are firm, rich and cakey rather than light and fluffy, due to the absence of egg whites in the mixture.

DESSERTS

Tangerine Sorbet

2 cups water
3/4 cup granulated sugar
2 cups tangerine juice
1 large egg white, beaten to a light foam

Make a simple syrup by dissolving the sugar and the water in a small saucepan and bringing it just to a boil over medium heat. Remove from the heat, cool and refrigerate until chilled. Combine the syrup with the tangerine juice and the egg white and freeze in an ice-cream maker according to the manufacturer's instructions. Set aside in a freezer container until you are ready to assemble the dessert.

Citrus Sauce

1/2 cup granulated sugar
2 tablespoons water
1/4 cup orange juice
2 tablespoons unsalted butter, softened
Zest of one orange, finely chopped

See page 139 for a description of making caramel, and proceed as directed, combining the sugar and the water in a small heavy saucepan and cooking the caramel to a golden brown. Add the orange juice (stand back as the mixture may splatter at this stage), stirring vigorously to mix in well, and deglaze the pan. Add the butter and the orange zest and stir constantly until the sauce is thickened and the butter has melted evenly. Set aside, covered, until you are ready to assemble the dessert.

SOMMELIER'S WINE CHOICE
Fonseca Vintage Port
Quinto do Noval Vintage Port

Chocolate Soufflés

3/4 cup unsalted butter, softened
2 tablespoons granulated sugar
5 1/2 ounces bittersweet chocolate, chopped into 1/2-inch pieces
3 large eggs
3 large egg yolks
1/4 cup plus 2 tablespoons granulated sugar
5 tablespoons all-purpose flour

Preheat the oven to 325 degrees F. Use some of the butter to thoroughly grease six 4-ounce ramekins, dust them with sugar, shaking out the excess, and set them aside in a shallow roasting pan.

In a dry small mixing bowl set over a saucepan of gently simmering water, combine the chocolate and the butter and remove from the heat. Stir until they are well mixed, melted and smooth. Let cool.

In the bowl of an electric mixer or with a whisk, beat the eggs, egg yolks and sugar together until the mixture is pale, fluffy and holds a ribbon. Add the flour and mix in well, scraping down the sides of the bowl as necessary. Add the melted chocolate mixture and mix on high speed for about 5 minutes more, until quite thick.

Spoon the mixture into the ramekins to fill them three-quarters of the way up, then carefully pour boiling water into the roasting pan to come halfway up the sides of the ramekins. Bake the soufflés in the oven for 18 to 20 minutes, or until they are just firm in the center and a toothpick comes out clean.

Assembly

2 teaspoons confectioners' sugar
6 pastry cups, available from better bakeries (optional)

Gently reheat the citrus sauce, swirling and stirring, but do not allow it to boil. Unmold 1 soufflé upside down onto each of 6 heated dessert plates, sprinkle a little powdered sugar over the top and place a scoop of tangerine sorbet in a pastry cup on the side, if desired, or directly onto the plate. Spoon some of the citrus sauce around the edge.

Lemon Sandwich

WITH CANDIED CITRUS ZEST AND STRAWBERRY SALAD

SERVES 4

At last, your chance to end the meal with a salad and a sandwich!

Candied Citrus Zest

1 cup water
1/3 cup granulated sugar
Zest of 3 oranges, cut into fine julienne strips
Zest of 2 lemons, cut into fine julienne strips

In a small saucepan, make a simple syrup by combining the water and sugar and stirring over medium heat until the sugar is completely dissolved. Add the citrus zest and increase the heat to medium, then simmer for 10 to 15 minutes, or until the zest is tender. Remove with a strainer and cool on waxed paper until you are ready to use.

Phyllo Wafers (for the sandwich)

1/4 pound frozen phyllo pastry, thawed for 30 minutes at room temperature
1/4 cup clarified butter (see page 136)
2 tablespoons ground almonds
2 tablespoons granulated sugar

Lightly oil a baking sheet and line it with parchment paper. Cover the pastry with a damp tea towel while you are working to prevent it from drying out. Carefully peel off 1 sheet of the pastry and lay it on a lightly floured work surface. Brush it with a little clarified butter, then sprinkle evenly with 2 teaspoons each of the ground almonds and the sugar. Repeat with 5 more sheets of phyllo, brushing each one with clarified butter and sprinkling with ground almonds and sugar, until you have an even pile of 6 sheets of pastry. Press down evenly to compact the pastry.

Using a 3-inch cookie cutter and a small knife, carefully cut out eight 3-inch circles and transfer them to the baking sheet. Lay another sheet of parchment paper over the top of the wafers and place another baking sheet of the same size over the top. Refrigerate for 1 hour.

SOMMELIER'S WINE CHOICE
Mumm Cuvée Napa Sparkling Wine (Napa Valley)
Far Niente "Dolce" (Napa Valley)

Lemon Cream

2 lemons, zest grated and reserved and juice squeezed
7/8 cup granulated sugar
3 eggs, well beaten
1 cup unsalted butter, cut into 8 pieces

In a medium heatproof mixing bowl, combine the lemon zest and juice, sugar, eggs and butter and whisk together until well blended. Set the bowl over a saucepan of gently simmering water and cook, stirring all the time, until the mixture has thickened to the consistency of heavy cream. Strain the mixture while it is still warm into another bowl and cover the surface of the cream with plastic wrap so that the plastic is touching the surface to prevent a skin from forming. Place in the freezer for 15 minutes to firm up before assembly.

Strawberry Purée and Salad

2 pints strawberries, stems removed
Granulated sugar, to taste (depending on the sweetness of the berries)
The reserved candied citrus zest

In a food processor fitted with the metal blade or in a blender, process 1 pint of the strawberries until puréed. Add sugar as needed (usually only 1 to 2 tablespoons). Set aside until needed. Quarter the remaining pint of strawberries and toss in a small mixing bowl with the citrus zest.

Assembly

Preheat the oven to 350 degrees F. Remove the phyllo wafers from the refrigerator and bake in the hot oven for 10 to 12 minutes, or until golden. Alllow to cool on a rack.

On each of 4 dessert plates, place 1 phyllo wafer and spoon about 3 tablespoons of the lemon cream in a mound in its center. Place another wafer over the top to create a sandwich. Drizzle a little of the strawberry purée around the edge of each sandwich and place a spoonful of the sliced strawberries and candied zest over the purée. Serve immediately, or the lemon cream will begin to run.

Banana Cream Pie

WITH CHOCOLATE SORBET

SERVES 4

My interpretation of an American classic, with a crisp almond-phyllo crust.

Cream Filling

1 large egg
1 large egg yolk
1/3 cup granulated sugar
1 tablespoon all-purpose flour
1 tablespoon cornstarch

1 cup milk
1/4 vanilla bean, halved lengthwise and
   seeds scraped out
1 cup heavy cream, whipped to soft peaks

In the bowl of an electric mixer or with a wire whisk, combine the egg, egg yolk, sugar, flour and cornstarch and beat together until very smooth. In a small saucepan, combine the milk with the vanilla bean and its seeds and bring to a simmer over low heat. Pour a little of the hot milk mixture into the egg mixture, whisking all the time, and then pour the egg mixture back into the saucepan with the remaining milk. Over medium-low heat, cook the mixture until it thickens, but do not allow it to boil. Strain through a fine sieve into a bowl, cover with plastic wrap touching the surface of the cream to prevent a skin from forming, and refrigerate until chilled. Fold in the whipped cream and return to the refrigerator.

Pie Shell

1/4 pound phyllo pastry, thawed for 30 minutes at room temperature
1/4 cup clarified butter (see page 136)
1/4 cup ground almonds
1/4 cup granulated sugar
2 cups dried white beans, for weighting the pie shell

Line a baking sheet with parchment paper and preheat the oven to 350 degrees F.

Cover the phyllo pastry with a damp tea towel while you are working with it to prevent it from drying out. Carefully peel off 1 sheet of the pastry and lay it on a lightly floured work surface. Brush it with a little clarified butter and sprinkle it with 2 teaspoons each of the ground almonds and the sugar. Lay another sheet of pastry on top and repeat the process, continuing until you have a stack of 6 sheets, each one brushed with butter and sprinkled with almonds and sugar. Roll the pastry lightly with a rolling pin to compact it.

Place four 4 1/2-inch ring molds or 4 disposable aluminum pie tins on the prepared baking sheet. Using a 5-inch cookie cutter, cut 4 circles of pastry that are 1/2 inch larger than the ring molds or the bases of the pie tins. Transfer the pastry circles to the molds, pressing each one into the bottom but

letting the pastry come partway up the inside of the mold or tin. Place a small circle of parchment inside each mold to protect the pastry from the beans, then fill the mold with the dried beans. Bake in the oven for about 15 minutes, until the pastry is golden brown, then remove the beans and allow the shells to cool.

Chocolate Sorbet

2 cups water
1 1/2 cups granulated sugar
1 tablespoon Dutch-process cocoa powder
7 ounces "couverture" or other high-quality dark bittersweet chocolate, chopped into small pieces

In a medium saucepan, combine the water and the sugar over medium-low heat and stir until the sugar is dissolved. Simmer the mixture very slowly for 1 hour, then stir in the cocoa powder. Put the chopped chocolate into a large mixing bowl and pour the cocoa syrup over it, stirring to mix until the chocolate has melted and the mixture is smooth. Refrigerate until chilled and then freeze in an ice-cream maker according to the manufacturer's instructions.

Assembly

Juice of 1 lemon
2 bananas
The pastry shells
The reserved cream filling

4 teaspoons raw sugar
1/2 cup crème anglaise (see page 136, optional)
2 ounces bittersweet chocolate, melted (optional)

Preheat a broiler to high heat. Fill a mixing bowl with cold water and add the lemon juice. Peel and slice the bananas 1/4 inch thick and put the slices into the acidulated water.

When ready to serve, drain the banana slices. Place the pastry shells on a broiler pan and spoon in some of the cream filling so that it fills each shell completely. Arrange the banana slices on the top in overlapping circles, covering the top of the pie and extending a little over the edge. Sprinkle 1 teaspoon of raw sugar evenly over each pie. Put the pies under the hot broiler and caramelize the raw sugar, turning the pies and watching carefully to see that they do not burn. Serve on chilled dessert plates with a scoop of chocolate sorbet on the side. If desired, spoon a little crème anglaise on the side of the plate and dot with a few drops of melted chocolate.

SOMMELIER'S WINE CHOICE
Château de Fargues Sauternes (Bordeaux)   Au Bon Climat "Thumbs Up" (Santa Barbara)

DESSERTS

Clafoutis
OF SUMMER PEACHES "PÈRE ANDRÉ"

SERVES 8

This classic French dessert comes from my father-in-law in Biarritz, owner of that town's most famous and respected pastry shop for more than 30 years.
He warned me, "This is better if you make it the day before and then warm it in a low oven just before serving. That way the flavors have a chance to mature."
Who am I to argue with my father-in-law?

Pastry

1 7/8 cups all-purpose flour
1/2 teaspoon salt
2 tablespoons vanilla sugar or granulated sugar
2/3 cup plus 1 tablespoon unsalted butter, chilled and cut into 1/2-inch pieces
1 large egg, lightly beaten
1 to 3 tablespoons ice water, as needed

In a food processor fitted with the metal blade, combine the flour, salt and vanilla and process until combined. Add the butter and pulse 3 or 4 times, until the butter is the size of large bread crumbs. Do not overprocess. Remove the cover and drizzle half the egg and 1 tablespoon of ice water over the surface, then pulse again for a few seconds. Add the remaining egg and 1 more tablespoon of ice water and process until the mixture comes together in a ball on the central column. This should happen within 5 to 10 seconds; if it does not, you may need to add an additional tablespoon of water (this will depend on the dryness of the flour). Turn the dough out onto a piece of plastic wrap, bring together into a ball and refrigerate for 1 to 2 hours to make it easier to roll out.

Butter and flour a 9-by-2-inch nonstick metal cake tin or springform pan. On a lightly floured work surface, roll out the dough 1/8 inch thick and line the prepared tin, building up the edges a little to stop the pastry from sagging down into the pan. Refrigerate the pie shell for 45 minutes.

Batter

4 large eggs
1/2 cup plus 1 tablespoon granulated sugar
1/2 cup heavy cream
1/2 cup milk
3 tablespoons all-purpose flour

In a blender, combine the eggs, sugar, cream, milk and flour and blend until smooth.

Cooking and Assembly

The prepared pie shell
2 cups dried white beans, for baking the pie shell
1/4 cup unsalted butter
5 large or 7 medium peaches, peeled, pitted and quartered
1/4 cup granulated sugar
The prepared batter

Preheat the oven to 350 degrees F. Prick the bottom of the pie shell and line it with a circle of parchment paper. Fill the shell with the beans and bake in the hot oven for 15 minutes, then remove the beans and paper.

Meanwhile, in a small sauté pan, melt the butter over medium heat and add the peaches and the sugar. Cook gently for 4 to 5 minutes, or until the peaches are tender and slightly caramelized. Pour a little of the batter into the pie shell and distribute the peaches evenly over the bottom.

Pour in the remaining batter and bake the clafoutis again for about 1 hour, or until the center is just firm. Cool on a rack and serve warm, or serve the next day.

SOMMELIER'S WINE CHOICE
Domaines Coyeaux Muscat de Baumes-de-Venise (Rhône)
Inniskillin "Ice Wine" (Niagara)

DESSERTS

Chocolate Croissant Pudding
WITH WILD TURKEY SAUCE

SERVES 6

People think of this as a spendthrift dish, but the inspiration was actually frugal. I was working at a restaurant where a lot of stale croissants were thrown out every morning, so I created this to make use of them. Think of it as a bread pudding.

Wild Turkey Sauce

1 cup milk
1/2 vanilla bean, halved lengthwise and seeds scraped out
4 large egg yolks
1/4 cup granulated sugar
1 tablespoon Wild Turkey liqueur, or to taste

In a small saucepan, combine the milk with the vanilla bean and seeds and bring just to a boil. Remove from the heat and allow to infuse for 5 minutes, then strain out the vanilla pod. In an electric mixer or with a whisk, beat the egg yolks together with the sugar until the mixture is pale and thickened. Pour about a quarter of the hot milk into the egg yolk mixture and mix until well combined, then return the yolk mixture to the pan with the rest of the milk and, over medium-low heat, stir continuously until thickened. Do not allow the mixture to boil. Strain it through a strainer into a clean pan and add Wild Turkey liqueur to taste. Cool the sauce and refrigerate, covered, until chilled.

Croissants

4 croissants, cut in half horizontally

Preheat the oven to 350 degrees F. On a baking sheet, toast the croissant halves until golden, about 8 to 10 minutes, watching carefully so that they do not burn. Remove from the oven and, when cool, break the croissants up into 1/2-inch pieces and set aside. Reduce the oven temperature to 350 degrees F.

Custard

2 cups heavy cream
1/4 vanilla bean, halved lengthwise and seeds scraped out
5 large egg yolks
1/4 cup plus 2 tablespoons sugar

In a medium saucepan, heat the cream and the vanilla bean together over medium-high heat. Bring the cream to just below boiling point, then remove it from the heat and allow to infuse for 5 minutes. Strain out the vanilla pod. In a medium mixing bowl, whisk the egg yolks and sugar together until the mixture is pale and thickened. Gradually whisk the warm cream into the egg yolks and then return the mixture to a clean saucepan. Over medium-low heat, bring the mixture up to just below a boil, stirring all the time until thickened, and immediately remove it from the heat.

Finishing

The reserved toasted croissant pieces
8 ounces bittersweet baking chocolate, cut into 1/2-inch chunks
1 tablespoon confectioners' sugar

Arrange an equal amount of toasted croissant pieces in each of six 8-ounce ramekins or ovenproof bowls. Distribute the chocolate chunks evenly among the ramekins. Spoon the warm custard over the mixture, pressing down with a fork to be sure all the pieces of croissant are soaked in the custard, and cover each ramekin tightly with aluminum foil.

Place the ramekins in a roasting pan and pour in enough very hot water to come halfway up their sides. Bake in the hot oven for 15 to 20 minutes, or until just set, then pierce the foil with a toothpick to release the steam and let stand for 5 minutes before removing the rest of the foil. (Note: At this stage you could cool and refrigerate the puddings for several hours or overnight. Warm them through in a 400-degree -F oven for 4 to 5 minutes before serving.)

When you are ready to serve, dust the top of each warm pudding with a little powdered sugar and serve the chilled sauce in a sauceboat on the side.

SOMMELIER'S CHOICE
A good espresso

DESSERTS

Crumble Berry Pie
WITH VANILLA ICE CREAM

SERVES 6

What goes best with mixed berries and streusel topping? Real vanilla-bean ice cream, of course.

Vanilla Bean Ice Cream

1 1/4 cups milk
1 1/4 cups heavy cream
1 vanilla bean, halved lengthwise and seeds scraped out
2/3 cup sugar
6 egg yolks

In a heavy saucepan, combine the milk, cream, vanilla bean and seeds and half of the sugar. Stirring constantly over medium heat until the sugar is dissolved, bring the mixture up almost to a boil and then remove from the heat. Allow to infuse for 1 to 2 minutes, then strain out the vanilla pod and seeds. In a large mixing bowl, combine the egg yolks with the remaining sugar and beat until pale, fluffy and the mixture holds a ribbon, about 3 to 4 minutes. Drizzle about 1/2 cup of the hot cream mixture into the egg yolks, beating all the time. When well blended, return the egg yolk mixture to the pan with the rest of the cream mixture and blend together well. Cook the mixture over low heat, stirring constantly, until it coats the back of the spoon and is the consistency of thick cream. Do not let it come to a boil. Cool the mixture by plunging the bottom of the saucepan into a bowl filled with ice water. When cool, freeze in an ice-cream maker according to the manufacturer's instructions.

Sugar Dough

3 1/2 cups all-purpose flour
1/2 cup granulated sugar
1/4 teaspoon baking powder
1 cup cold unsalted butter, cut into 1/2-inch pieces
1 large egg, lightly beaten
1 to 2 tablespoons ice water, as needed

Follow the method for sugar dough in Strawberry Rhubarb Pie on page 125.

SOMMELIER'S WINE CHOICE
Tokaji Aszu "3 puttonyos" (Hungary)
Trimbach Riesling "Vendange Tardive" (Alsace)

Almond Cream

Follow the method for almond cream in Strawberry Rhubarb Pie on page 125.

Crumble Dough

1/2 cup unsalted butter, cut into 1/2-inch cubes
1/2 cup granulated sugar
1/4 teaspoon vanilla extract
1 cup all-purpose flour

In a medium mixing bowl, cut the butter and sugar together with a pastry cutter or 2 knives until the mixture resembles coarse bread crumbs. Add the vanilla and the flour and blend together until the flour is evenly distributed and the dough is solid. Wrap with plastic wrap, label (to distinguish it from the sugar dough) and refrigerate for 1 hour.

Cooking and Assembly

1 1/2 cups fresh blackberries
1 1/2 cups fresh raspberries
1 1/2 cups fresh blueberries
Granulated sugar, to taste (depending on the sweetness of the berries)
6 sprigs fresh mint, for garnish

Preheat the oven to 350 degrees F. Gently mix the berries all together in a bowl and add sugar to taste.

Remove the sugar dough from the refrigerator and roll out on a lightly floured surface to a thickness of 1/8 inch and use it to line six 5-inch tart shells. Refrigerate the shells for 20 minutes, then prick the bottoms of the shells and spread a layer of almond cream 1/4 inch thick in the bottom of each shell.

Bake in the oven for 12 to 15 minutes, or until the filling is slightly golden and firm. Remove the pies and set on a rack for 15 minutes to cool, then fill them with the berry mixture. Using the large holes of a grater, grate the crumble dough over the pies. Return the pies to the 350-degree -F oven for 30 minutes, or until the crumble topping is golden brown. Serve the warm pies on individual dessert plates with a scoop of vanilla ice cream on the side and garnish with a sprig of mint.

DESSERTS

11:00 p.m.

At last the day is ending. One by one the waiters leave as their tables clear and the last customers go home. New big stockpots are being put on a range for tomorrow's sauces. *Tomato skins* are going into a low oven to crisp overnight. The dishwashers are finishing up and putting the sets of dishes away.

The line chefs change out of their dirty whites and clock out. They've been on their feet continuously for almost seven hours. It's never easy to meet the standards of an exacting kitchen, but it's a hell of a challenge. And everyone here will be back tomorrow, eager to do it all over again.

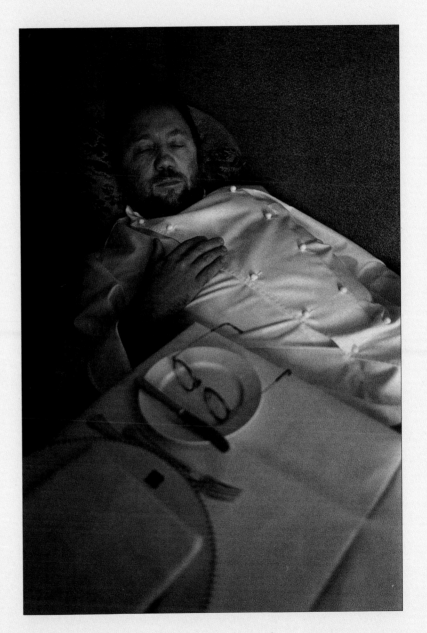

Basic Recipes

Chicken Stock

1 1/2 quarts water
5 pounds uncooked chicken carcasses, wings
   or assorted pieces
2 whole carrots, washed but unpeeled
2 whole ribs celery, washed

1 whole leek
1 medium yellow onion, peeled
1/2 head unpeeled garlic
10 white peppercorns, lightly crushed
1 sprig thyme

In a large stockpot, combine the water and chicken pieces and bring to a slow simmer over medium heat. Skim the impurities from the surface with a large flat spoon, then add the carrots, celery, leek, onion, garlic, peppercorns and thyme and simmer, partially covered and undisturbed, for 5 hours, adding a little more water if necessary to make sure that the water level doesn't fall below the level of the bones. Strain the stock through a strainer lined with a double thickness of slightly dampened cheesecloth, allow to cool and refrigerate overnight. Skim off the fat from the top of the stock and use as directed, or freeze for future sauces. *Note*: If you have a large stockpot, you can double, or even triple, this recipe.

Clarified Butter

YIELD: JUST OVER 3/4 CUP

1/2 pound unsalted butter, at room temperature

In a heavy saucepan, melt 1/2 pound of unsalted butter over low heat, without stirring or disturbing the pan. Turn off the heat, and with a large flat spoon, gently skim off the white froth that rises to the top. Carefully pour the clear yellow "clarified" butter into a container, leaving behind the milky white residue at the bottom of the pan. Clarified butter is awkward to make in lesser quantity than 1/2 pound, but it will keep, covered, in the refrigerator for 2 to 3 weeks.

Crème Anglaise

YIELD: 1 1/2 CUPS

1 cup milk
1/2 vanilla bean, halved lengthwise and seeds scraped out
4 large egg yolks
1/4 cup granulated sugar

In a small saucepan, combine the milk with the vanilla bean and seeds and bring just to a boil. Remove from the heat and allow to infuse for 5 minutes, then strain out the vanilla pod and seeds. In an electric mixer or with a whisk, beat the egg yolks together with the sugar until the mixture is pale and thickened. Pour about a quarter of the hot milk into the egg-yolk mixture and mix until well combined. Then return the yolk mixture to the pan with the rest of the milk and, over medium-low heat, stir continuously until thickened. Do not allow the mixture to boil. Strain into a bowl, let stand for 5 minutes, then cover the sauce with plastic wrap so that the plastic is touching the surface, to prevent a skin from forming. Refrigerate the sauce until chilled.

Duck, Lamb, Chicken or Squab Jus

YIELD: ABOUT 1 CUP

1 tablespoon extra virgin olive oil
1 to 2 pounds duck, lamb, chicken or squab carcasses
   or bones, chopped into approximately 2-inch pieces
1 small carrot, coarsely chopped
1/2 small yellow onion, coarsely chopped

2 cloves unpeeled garlic, crushed with
   a chef's knife
1 sprig fresh thyme
1/2 cup white wine
2 cups chicken stock (see left)

Preheat the oven to 350 degrees F. On top of the stove, heat a heavy roasting or braising pan over medium-high heat. Add the oil and the carcass pieces to the pan and stir over the heat for 3 to 4 minutes, or until just browned. Put the pan in the oven and roast for 15 minutes, stirring halfway through the cooking time. Add the carrot, onion and garlic to the pan and roast for 15 minutes more, or until the vegetables and bones are well caramelized. On top of the stove over medium heat, add the thyme and the wine and deglaze the pan, stirring and scraping the bottom and sides to release all of the flavorful bits into the liquid, and continue to cook until the wine has almost completely evaporated. Add the stock and simmer, stirring occasionally, until it has reduced by about half so that about 1 cup of liquid remains. Remove from the heat and strain through a strainer lined with a double thickness of slightly dampened cheesecloth, pressing down on the solids to extract all their flavor. Discard the solids. Use as directed in the recipe or freeze for future sauces.

Basic Recipes

Lobster Nage

YIELD: 1 1/3 CUPS

This recipe for lobster stock yields about 1 quart. In order to make the finished lobster nage, you will only need 5 ounces of the stock. The remaining stock can be refrigerated for up to 3 days or, if you like, frozen in 5-ounce quantities for future sauces.

LOBSTER STOCK

YIELD: 1 QUART

Shells from 2 lobsters
1 cup white wine
1/4 cup brandy
1 tablespoon unsalted butter
1 rib celery, roughly chopped
1/4 medium yellow onion, roughly chopped
1/2 leek, white part only, roughly chopped

1 medium carrot, roughly chopped
2 cloves unpeeled garlic
1 sprig fresh parsley
1 teaspoon tomato paste
2 plum tomatoes, halved
1 sprig of fresh thyme
8 cups water

Preheat an oven to 350 degrees F and place a large roasting pan in it to heat up. In a heavy muslin bag, crush the lobster shells with a hammer or heavy rolling pin, or coarsely grind them in a food processor. Place the lobster shells (without the bag) in the hot roasting pan and roast for 20 minutes, turning them over halfway through the cooking time. On top of the stove, add the wine and brandy and deglaze the pan, stirring and scraping the bottom and sides to release all the flavorful bits into the liquid. Set aside.

In a large saucepan or stockpot, melt the butter over medium heat and add the celery, onion, leek, carrot, garlic and parsley. Sauté the vegetables, stirring often, for about 6 to 8 minutes, or until they are just golden. Add the roasted lobster shells with their deglazing liquid and cook for 1 to 2 minutes, or until most of the liquid has evaporated. Add the tomato paste and cook for 2 minutes more, then add the tomatoes, thyme and water and stir to mix thoroughly. Bring the stock to a simmer and skim off any impurities. Reduce the heat to low and cook, uncovered, for 3 hours, adding water as necessary to keep the shells covered by 1 inch.

Strain the stock through a strainer lined with a double thickness of slightly dampened cheesecloth into a clean pan, pressing down hard on the solids to be sure you extract all the flavor from them. Discard the solids. Over medium heat, reduce the stock again by about half, or until about 1 quart of stock remains.

FINISHING

2/3 cup lobster stock, as above
2/3 cup unsalted butter, at room temperature, cut into 6 equal pieces
Salt and cayenne pepper

At serving time, when you are ready to finish the nage, bring the stock to a boil, then reduce the heat to low. Add 2 pieces of the butter, stir until melted and bring back to a simmer, then pour the nage into a blender. Blend at high speed, removing the lid to gradually add the remaining 4 pieces of butter and blend just until thoroughly emulsified. Season to taste with salt and pepper and pour into a measuring cup with a lip, then skim off any foam that rises to the top. Use within a hour. To reheat, if cold: Bring the nage back to a simmer and blend again for 10 to 15 seconds to re-emulsify.

Vegetable Nage

YIELD: 1 1/3 CUPS

This recipe yields about 1 1/2 quarts of vegetable stock. In order to make the finished butter nage, you will only need 5 ounces of the stock. The remaining stock can be chilled for up to 3 days or, if you like, frozen in 5-ounce quantities for future sauces.

VEGETABLE STOCK

YIELD: 1 1/2 QUARTS

1 tablespoon unsalted butter
10 ribs celery, coarsely chopped
1 large white onion, coarsely chopped
2 leeks, white part only, coarsely chopped
1 sprig fresh thyme

6 cloves unpeeled garlic
1 sprig fresh parsley
1 quart white wine
1 quart water

In a large saucepan, melt the butter over low heat and add the vegetables and herbs. Sweat the mixture over medium-low heat, stirring occasionally, for about 30 minutes, or until the vegetables are completely translucent and almost broken down. Be sure not to let them brown at all, otherwise the sauce will not be perfectly white. Add wine, increase the heat slightly, and simmer gently for 1 hour. Add the water and simmer gently for an additional 20 minutes. Strain the stock through a sieve, pressing down hard on the solids to be sure you extract all the flavor from them. Discard the vegetables and set the stock aside. Measure 2/3 cup vegetable stock into a medium saucepan and chill or freeze the remaining stock (see headnote).

FINISHING

2/3 cup vegetable stock, as above
3/4 cup unsalted butter, at room temperature, cut into 6 equal pieces
Salt and freshly ground white pepper

At serving time, when you are ready to finish the nage, bring the stock to a boil, then reduce the heat to low. Add one-third of the butter, stir until melted, then pour the nage into a blender. Blend at high speed, removing the lid to gradually add the remaining 4 pieces of butter and blend just until thoroughly emulsified. Season to taste with salt and pepper and use as directed in the recipe. Use within half an hour. To reheat, if cold: Bring the nage back to a simmer and blend again for 10 to 15 seconds to re-emulsify.

Basic Recipes

Red Wine Sauce

2 tablespoons unsalted butter
1/2 pound shallots, thinly sliced
1 tablespoon whole white peppercorns,
    lightly crushed

1 cup port
2 quarts red wine
2 quarts veal stock

In a large stockpot, heat the butter over medium-high heat and add the shallots and peppercorns. Cook, stirring occasionally, for about 10 minutes or until caramelized. Add the port and simmer until it is almost completely evaporated. Add the red wine and again reduce until almost completely gone. Add the veal stock and reduce by half, until 1 quart of liquid remains. Pass the sauce through a fine strainer and use as directed or freeze in 1/2-cup quantities for future sauces.

Roasted Garlic

20 cloves peeled garlic
2 tablespoons extra virgin olive oil
Salt and freshly ground white pepper

Preheat an oven to 350 degrees F. In a mixing bowl, toss together the garlic, oil and salt and pepper. Place the garlic in the center of a 12-inch-long piece of aluminum foil, fold in the long ends and fold together at the top to create a seal. Fold in the short ends to create a secure packet. On a baking sheet, roast the packet for 20 minutes, then turn over, cut a small steam vent in the underside, and roast the packet upside down for a further 10 minutes. Use as directed or refrigerate in the foil for up to 1 week.

Roasted Shallots

20 unpeeled shallots
3 tablespoons extra virgin olive oil
Salt and freshly ground white pepper

Preheat an oven to 350 degrees F. In a mixing bowl, toss together the shallots, olive oil and salt and pepper to taste. Place the shallots in the center of a 14-inch-long piece of aluminum foil, fold in the long ends and fold together at the top to create a seal. Fold in the short ends to create a secure packet. On a baking sheet, roast the packet for 30 minutes, then turn to the other side, cut a small steam vent in the underside, and roast the packet upside down for a further 10 minutes. Let cool and then slip the shallots out of their skins. Use as directed or refrigerate in the foil for up to 1 week.

Veal Stock

10 pounds veal knucklebones
4 medium carrots, washed but unpeeled, cut into 1-inch pieces
2 medium yellow onions, cut into 1-inch pieces
1 cup tomato paste
3 1/2 cups dry white wine

Preheat an oven to 400 degrees F. In a large roasting pan, roast the veal bones for 1 1/2 hours, turning them over once. Add the carrots and onions, stir together and roast for a further 45 minutes, or until the bones and vegetables are browned. Stir the tomato paste into the mixture and roast for 5 minutes more, then transfer all the solids to a large stockpot and pour off and discard the fat from the roasting pan. Add the wine to the roasting pan and deglaze it over medium heat, stirring and scraping the bottom and sides to release all the flavorful bits into the liquid. Pour the wine over the bones and vegetables in the stockpot and add enough water to cover them by 4 inches. Bring to a simmer over low heat, cover, and simmer for 10 hours, skimming off the fats and impurities as necessary. If the water level falls too low, add more water so that at the end of the cooking time the bones are still covered by 2 inches of liquid. Strain the liquid into a clean saucepan and reduce over medium heat until 3 quarts of liquid remain.

Reduced Veal Stock (Demi-Glace)

Reduce 3 quarts of veal stock until only 1 1/2 quarts of liquid remain. Use as directed or freeze in small quantities for future sauces.

Techniques

Caramel

In a heavy pan with a tight-fitting lid, combine the water and granulated sugar over medium heat until the sugar has dissolved and the liquid is completely clear. Increase the heat to high and boil the syrup, covered and without stirring, until the bubbles thicken (you will have to peek occasionally). Remove the lid and continue boiling until the syrup begins to turn golden. At this stage, you can swirl the pan occasionally to help the caramel cook evenly. Cook the syrup until it is a light brown color, then remove from the heat and continue swirling the pan. The caramel will continue to cook for another minute after you remove it from the heat, and you do not want it to burn. (*Note*: If you will be adding another liquid to the caramel, cook it until it is dark golden brown. When you add the additional liquid, it will stop the caramel cooking immediately.) When the syrup has reached the desired color, cool the base of the pan in a bowl of cold water to stop the cooking. Be careful when working with caramel, as it gets very, very hot.

Chiffonade of Herbs

(use for mint and basil only)
Pile up several herb leaves, roll them into a cigar shape, and slice thinly across the leaves. Use a sharp knife, otherwise you will bruise the leaves and they will turn brown.

Cleaning and Preparing Sculpin Fish

Sculpin is a West Coast fish that is related to rockfish (also called Pacific Ocean perch or redfish). You must be very careful in cleaning sculpin: across the top of the spine between the gills are numerous spines that are poisonous and can cause severe infection. Have your fishmonger prepare the fish as directed below, or wear rubber gloves while cleaning it and be sure to avoid touching the ends of the spines.

Using kitchen shears and a boning knife, remove the fins, gills and sharp spines from the back, sides and belly of the fish. Make a shallow cut along each side of the backbone from head to tail and snip through the backbone at the very top just behind the head and at the very bottom just above the tail. Working the boning knife down along the ribcage on either side, remove the backbone, ribs and intestines through this opening, leaving the belly of the fish intact.

To Peel and Devein Shrimp

Pinch off the tail of the shrimp at the very bottom, then peel off a round or two of the shell from the underside. The shrimp should then just pop out of the remaining shell. If the intestinal vein is dark, pull it, with the aid of a paper towel, out through the head end of the shrimp. If it is not too dark, there is no need to remove it, and certainly no need to cut into the body of the shrimp to get it out.

Peeling, Seeding and Cutting Tomatoes

Bring a generous amount of water to a boil in a saucepan. Cut a shallow cross in the base of each tomato and plunge the tomatoes, not more than 4 at a time, into the boiling water. After about 15 seconds, remove them with a skimmer or slotted spoon to a bowl of ice water to stop the cooking. Using a small paring knife, peel each tomato skin away, beginning at the cross in the bottom, then quarter the tomato lengthwise and scrape out the seeds with a teaspoon. Chop the flesh as directed in the recipe.

To Trim Artichokes into Bottoms

Have ready a large bowl of cold water into which you have dropped the 2 halves of a lemon and their juice. Break off the stem of the artichoke. Holding the artichoke bottom up, bend the lower leaves back on themselves, one at a time, until they snap, then peel them off toward the base. Continue until the pale inner leaves are exposed, then cut off the remaining pale leaves just at the top of the base.

With a small sharp knife, trim off all the tough dark fibers that were left when you snapped off the leaves, trimming around in a circle, without removing too much of the flesh. If desired, trim with a vegetable peeler to make a smooth surface. With a teaspoon, scrape out the choke and any remaining leaves. Drop the trimmed bottom into the acidulated water and repeat the process with the remaining artichokes.

Working with Truffles

Run fresh truffles under running water and brush them very gently with a soft-bristled brush. Canned truffles do not need to be rinsed, and *always* save the jus (or juices) for sauces. At Patina we use only imported truffles, either black or white. It is also possible to buy small cans of truffle jus, without a truffle. This is useful to have on hand when using fresh truffles or for added flavor when truffles are not available.

Metric Conversions

Liquid Weights

U.S. Measurements	Metric Equivalents
1/4 teaspoon	1.23 ml
1/2 teaspoon	2.5 ml
3/4 teaspoon	3.7 ml
1 teaspoon	5 ml
1 dessertspoon	10 ml
1 tablespoon (3 teaspoons)	15 ml
2 tablespoons (1 ounce)	30 ml
1/4 cup	60 ml
1/3 cup	80 ml
1/2 cup	120 ml
2/3 cup	160 ml
3/4 cup	180 ml
1 cup (8 ounces)	240 ml
2 cups (1 pint)	480 ml
3 cups	720 ml
4 cups (1 quart)	1 litre
4 quarts (1 gallon)	3 3/4 litres

Dry Weights

U.S. Measurements	Metric Equivalents
1/4 ounce	7 grams
1/3 ounce	10 grams
1/2 ounce	14 grams
1 ounce	28 grams
1 1/2 ounces	42 grams
1 3/4 ounces	50 grams
2 ounces	57 grams
3 ounces	85 grams
3 1/2 ounces	100 grams
4 ounces (1/4 pound)	114 grams
6 ounces	170 grams
8 ounces (1/2 pound)	227 grams
9 ounces	250 grams
16 ounces (1 pound)	464 grams
1.1 pounds	500 grams
2.2 pounds	1,000 grams

Temperatures

Fahrenheit	Celsius (Centigrade)
32° F (water freezes)	0° C
200° F	95° C
212° F (water boils)	100° C
225° F	110° C
250° F	120° C
275° F	135° C
300° F (slow oven)	150° C
325° F	160° C
350° F (moderate oven)	175° C
375° F	190° C
400° F (hot oven)	205° C
425° F	220° C
450° (very hot oven)	230° C
475° F	245° C
500° F (extremely hot oven)	260° C

Length

U.S. Measurements	Metric Equivalents
1/8 inch	3 mm
1/4 inch	6 mm
3/8 inch	1 cm
1/2 inch	12 mm
3/4 inch	2 cm
1 inch	2.5 cm
2 inches	5 cm
3 inches	7.5 cm
4 inches	10 cm
5 inches	12.5 cm

Approximate Equivalents

1 kilo is slightly more than 2 pounds
1 liter is slightly more than 1 quart
1 deciliter is slightly less than 1/2 cup
1 meter is slightly over 3 feet
1 centiliter is approximately 2 teaspoons
1 centimeter is approximately 3/8 inch

Resources

Caviar House
170 Lombard Street, San Francisco, CA 94111
415-693-9496 Fax: 415-693-0685
Caviar

D'Artagnan
399-419 St. Paul Avenue, Jersey City, NJ 07306
800-327-8246 Fax: 201-792-6113
Partridge, game birds, venison, duck liver (foie gras)

Gourmand
5873 Blackweider, Culver City, CA 90230
310-839-9222 Fax: 310-839-9155
Reggiano Parmesan, oils, specialty items

Mutual Trading Company
431 Crocker Street, Los Angeles, CA 90013
213-626-9458
Mandolines (called the Benriner Cutter, stock # 91572)

New Zealand Gourmet
371 N. Oak Street, Inglewood, CA 90303
310-677-7866 Fax: 310 -677-6137
Venison

Porcelaines Bernardaud
41 Madison Avenue, New York, NY 10010
212-696-2431
Limoges dinnerware

Special Foods
6533 S. Sepulveda Blvd., Los Angeles, CA 90045
310-641-0443 Fax: 310-641-0530
Fresh seafood, Santa Barbara shrimp, specialty items

United Poultry
736 North Broadway, Los Angeles, CA 90012
213-617-8522
Free-range chickens, squab, ducks, whole suckling pigs, fresh seafood

Urbani Truffles USA
29-24 40th Avenue, Long Island City, NY 11101
800-5ur-bani Fax: 718-392-1704
Fresh black and white truffles in season, truffle jus, truffle oil, canned black truffles

Van Rex/Surfas
8825 National Blvd., Culver City, CA 90232
310-559-4770 Fax: 310-559-4983
Mandolines (metal), specialty food and equipment items, oils, grains, chocolate, etc.

Acknowledgments

My deepest appreciation to all the employees at Patina who helped make this great adventure possible.

Executive Chef
William J. Fernow

Sous-Chefs
Ron Baker

Stephen Janke

Alec Lestr

Chefs de Cuisine Emeritus
Octavio Becerra, chef/partner, Pinot Bistro, Los Angeles
Traci Des Jardins, chef, Rubicon Restaurant, San Francisco

Kitchen

Jose M. Ambriz	Elli Dushane	Jose Hernandez	Martin Perez	Miguel J. Rodriguez	Andrew T. Warner
Manuel Arenas	Erik Fisher	Francisco Herrera	Michael J. Plapp	Salvador Rodriguez	Mariano Vargas
Ruben Arredondo	John Gadau	Eric Johnson	Carlos Antonio Ramirez	Christian A. Shaffer	Antonio Zavala
Peter A. Cossio	Guy Goldschmidt	Maximino Martinez	Conrado Reyes	Matthew Sullivan	Miguel Zavala
Bradley Cristea	Sergio Guiza	Julio E. Medrano	Federico Rodarte	Jim Switzenberg	Alejandro Zenteno
Mark C. Dunn	Rodolfo Gutirrez	William Mooney	Fernando Rodriguez	Andrea Tamburini	

Pastry
Victor Cordes, pastry chef

Mary Cooke

Jerry Del Rosario

Javier Franco

Gerald Hosl

Dining Room Manager
Gary L. Gotcher

Servers
Jeffrey Bamberger

Mark Borchetta

David P. Comegys III

Larry Kless

Charles Leon

William Priestly

Annie N. Rush

Back Waiters
Thomas Bicanic

Armando R. Gonzales

Laurent Sadou

Hostesses
Amy L. Alexander

Lisa Davenport

Jeannie M. Tsao

Julie Van Dam

Eva Nicole Whitacre

Bussers
Jose Santos Arredondo

Primitibo Arredondo

Israel Cornejo

Julio Guzman

Manuel Guzman

Isaias Morales

Jose Luis Ramos

Miguel Romo-Cruz

Bar
Thomas Dries

Christopher Forfar

John A. McKeel

Administration
Sheila Melanie Berrei

Tomas Claudio

Nina Crowe

Karen De Mille

Wesley Samuels

Eileen Wolf

Dishwashers
Miguel Almanza

Jorge Arredondo

Javier Gutierrez

Sergio Jiminez

Juan Juarez

Julio Juarez

Manuel Lemus

Benigno Moreno

Victor Rodriguez

Edgar F. Santiago

Francisco Zavala

Rafael Zavala

Maintenance
Refugio Ulloa

Index

A

Ahi Tuna Tower, 15
almond cream, 125, 134
A Potato Soup Like the Old Days with Flaky
   Potato Knish, 63
appetizers, cold
   ahi tuna and vegetables, 15
   artichoke terrine, 21-22
   corn, potato and frisée salad, 23
   crab salad, 16
   lobster salad, 19
   potato chips and smoked sturgeon, 17
appetizers, hot
   artichokes, roasted, 39
   artichoke "wienerschnitzel," 57
   calves' brains, 45
   chicken quesadillas, 48
   chicken wings, roasted, 37
   duck liver, sautéed, 50
   lobster, with white beans, 41
   portobello mushrooms, 54-55
   potato cannelloni, 36
   potato and forest mushroom lasagna, 42
   potato oyster ravioli, 40
   sardines "a Day in Nice," 46
   scallop rolls, 49
   sculpin, baked, 38
   shrimp
     with mashed potato and potato truffle
      chips, 34
     with polenta and pancetta, 44
   sweetbreads club sandwich, 56
   zucchini flowers, stuffed, 52
artichoke
   baby, 45, 99
   with calves' brains, 45
   mousse, 22
   terrine, 21
   to trim into bottoms, 139
   "wienerschnitzel" of, 57
Artichokes, Roasted, with Sea Scallops, Summer
   Truffles and Mizuna, 39
arugula, 17, 19, 39, 55, 75
asparagus, 19, 44, 95, 99
avocado, 15, 48

B

bacon, apple-smoked, sauce, 56
Banana Cream Pie with Chocolate Sorbet, 130
basil oil, 21
bean(s)
   dried white, 41
   fava, 19, 95, 99

   yellow wax, 99
   see also haricots verts
beef, filet (tenderloin), roasted, 106
beet greens, 75
bell peppers, 15, 99
beurre noisette, 84
blackberries, in crumble berry pie, 134
blueberries, in crumble berry pie, 134
bok choy, 85
bolognese, lobster, 76
bourbon. *See* liqueur; Wild Turkey
brains, calves, 45
brandade, of whitefish, 83
brioche, for club sandwich, 56
broth, chicken, 117
   see also stock
brunoise, 76, 79
butter
   clarified, 36, 49, 84, 102, 128, 130
     to make, 136
   horseradish, 84
   thyme lemon, 117
   vinaigrette of brown, 49

C

cabbage, white, 114
Calves' Brains with Sautéed Baby Artichokes
   and Balsamic Vinegar, 45
cannelloni, potato, 36
caramel, to make, 139
carrot(s)
   baby, 19, 80, 95, 99
   rounds, 117
   threads, 117
caviar, osetra, 19
celery, with rockfish, 73
celery root
   chips, 105
   mousse, 105
cheese
   Monterey Jack, 48
   Parmesan, 77
chicken
   breast, roasted, 117-18
   broth, 117
   fat, 36
   jus, 136
   liver, 37, 56
   quesadillas, 48
   stock, 136
   thighs, grilled, 48
   wings, roasted, 37
Chicken Breast, Roasted Farm, with
   Carrot Rounds and Fresh Thyme
   Lemon Sauce, 117-18

Chicken Quesadillas with Avocado and
   Cilantro Salsa, 48
Chicken Wings, Roasted, with Unorthodox
   Chopped Liver, 37
chiffonade, to cut, 139
chili peppers, 48
chips
   celery root, 105
   potato, 17, 49, 101
   potato truffle, 34
chive
   sauce, 42
   vinaigrette, 57
chocolate
   crème brûlée, 124
   Croissant Pudding with Wild Turkey Sauce, 132
   custard, 124
   sorbet, 130
   soufflés, 126
citrus sauce, 126
Clafoutis of Summer Peaches *Père*
   André, 131
Cold Spring Pea Soup with Yogurt, Crushed
   White Pepper and Mint, 64
confit
   duck, 36, 101
   in sauce, 101
   squab, 54, 101
corn
   crème brûlée, 124
   salad, with sautéed potato and frisée, 23
cornmeal. *See* polenta
cream
   almond, 125, 134
   filling, for banana pie, 130
   lemon, 128
créme
   anglaise, 130, 136
   brûlée
     chocolate, 124
     corn, 124
     galanga, 124
     vanilla, 124
   fraîche, 63
     and horseradish sauce, 17
     and lemon dressing, 19
     and mustard sauce, 16
croissant, to use stale, 132
croutons, 81
   chopped liver, 37
Crumble Berry Pie with Vanilla Ice Cream, 134
curly endive. *See* frisée
curry, lobster, 74
curry paste, Thai red, 74

custard, 132
   chocolate, 124

D

demi-glace, 138
desserts
   banana cream pie, 130
   chocolate
     croissant pudding, 132
     soufflés, 126
   clafoutis, 131
   crèmes brûlées, quartet of, 124
   crumble berry pie, 134
   lemon sandwich, 128
   strawberry rhubarb pie, 125
   see also ice cream; sorbet
dough. *See* pastry
dressing, crème fraîche and lemon, 19
duck
   confit, 36, 101
   fat, 36, 54, 84
   jus, 113, 136
   liver
     with croutons, 37
     with partridge, 114
     with squab, 101
     with squab and mushrooms, 55
     with sweetbreads, 56
   roasted, 113
   salad, 113 *(headnote)*
Duck Liver, Sautéed, with Caramelized Mango
   and Ginger, 50
Duck, Roasted, with Braised Figs in Port Wine
   Sauce, 113
Dungeness Crab Salad with Shoestring Potatoes
   and Two-Mustard Sauce, 16

E

Everything from a Rabbit with Polenta Gnocchi
   and Zucchini Mousse, 97-98

F

fat. *See* chicken; duck
fennel
   with rockfish, 73
   with sardines, 46
figs, with roast duck, 113
Filet of Beef, Roasted in Herb Crust, with Forest
   Mushroom Ragoût, 106

fish
   ahi tuna
     peppered tournedos of, 85
     and vegetables, 15

Index

halibut, roasted, 84
John Dory with truffle oil, 75
rockfish, roasted whole, 73
salmon, lasagna, 79
sardines, niçoise, with fennel, 46
sculpin, 38
  to clean, 139
sea bass, with lentils, 80-81
sturgeon, smoked, with potato chips, 17
whitefish, seared, 83
foie gras, 101
see also duck liver
"French fries," 83
frisée (curly endive), 16, 23

G

galanga, crème brûlée, 124
game
  partridge, roasted, 114
  pheasant, 119
  see also venison
garlic
  purée of quadruple-blanched, 80
  roasted, 22, 103, 106
  to roast, 138
ginger, candied fresh, 50
  see also galanga
gnocchi, polenta, 97

H

Halibut, Roasted Middle Piece of, with Fresh
  Horseradish Butter, 84
ham hock, 41
haricots verts, 19, 95, 99
herb crust, for beef, 106
High Cholesterol Foie Gras with Butter Potato
  Chips and Squab Confit Sauce, 101
horseradish
  butter, 84
  sauce, 17

I

ice cream, vanilla-bean, 134

J

John Dory with Truffle Oil, Braised Onions,
  Salsify and Bitter Greens, 75
jus
  chicken, 136
  duck, 113, 136
  lamb, 102, 136
  lobster, 76
  mushroom, 55
  potato, 83

rabbit, 97
  shrimp tarragon, 44
squab, 54, 136
truffle, 39, 52

K

kale, baby, 75
knishes, potato, 63

L

lamb
  jus, 102, 136
  loin, 103
  rack, roast medallions of, 102-103
lasagna
  potato and forest mushroom, 42
  salmon, 79
Layer cake of Odd Potato Chips and Smoked
  Sturgeon with Horseradish Sauce, 17
leeks, fried, 34
lemon
  cream, 128
  and crème fraîche dressing, 19
  sandwich, 128
  and thyme butter, 117
  zest, candied, 128
lemon grass
  with lobster, 74
  substitute for, 74
Lemon Sandwich with Candied Citrus Zest and
  Strawberry Salad, 128
lentils, 80
lettuce, oak leaf, 17, 19, 22, 39
liqueur, Wild Turkey, 132
liver
  chicken, 56, 101
    on croutons, 37
  duck, 50, 55, 56, 101, 114
    on croutons, 37

M

Maine Lobster "Harahan" with White Bean
  Mousse and Ham Hocks, 41
Maine Lobster "Return from Thailand," 74
Maine Lobster Risotto with Lobster
  Bolognese, 75-77
Maine Lobster Salad with Lemon Crème Fraîche,
  Spring Vegetables and Osetra Caviar, 19
mango, caramelized, 50
Medallions of Rack of Lamb, Roasted, with Fresh
  Peas, Pearl Onions, Chanterelle Mushrooms
  and Roasted Yukon Potatoes, 102-103
mizuna greens, 17, 22, 39, 55
mousse
  artichoke, 22

celery root, 105
tomato, 15, 22
white bean, 41
zucchini, 38, 52, 97
mushroom(s)
  black trumpet, 106
  cèpes, 106
  chanterelle, 42, 95, 102, 103, 106
  jus, 55
  morel, 106
  oyster, 42, 106
  porcini, 42
  portobello, 54
  ragoût, 103, 106
  shiitake, 36, 42, 98, 106
  white domestic, 42, 106
mustard, and crème fraîche sauce, 16
mustard greens, 75

N

nage
  butter sauce, 137
  lobster, 34, 137
  vegetable, 42, 137

O

Odd Potato Plaques with Salmon in Lasagna
  Form and Littleneck Clam "Vinaigrette," 79
oil
  basil, 21
  hazelnut, 23
  walnut, 23, 54
  white truffle, 75
olives, niçoise, 46
onions
  braised, 75
  pearl, 75, 80, 102, 114
orange
  sauce, 126
  zest, candied, 128
Osso Bucco "Summertime," 99

P

pancetta, 44
parsnips, fried, 114
Partridge, Roasted, with Cabbage, Pearl Onions,
  Apple-Smoked Bacon and Fried Parsnips, 114
pastry
  for clafoutis, 131
  crumble, 134
  cups, 126
  phyllo. *See* phyllo
  prepared puff, for potato knishes, 63
  sugar, for pie shell, 125, 134

peaches, in clafoutis, 131
pea(s)
  fresh, 19, 95
  frozen, 65
  ragoût of, with chanterelles, 103
  soup, cold, 65
  split, in soup, 65
pea tendrils, 74
pepper, black, sauce of, 105
Peppered Tournedos of Tuna with Bok Choy
  and Ponzu Sauce, 85
persimmons, with venison, 105
Pheasant, with Caramelized Salsify and
  Banyuls Sauce, 119
phyllo pastry
  for pie shell, 130
  wafers of, 128
pie
  banana cream, 130
  crumble berry, 134
  shell. *See* dough
  strawberry rhubarb, 125
polenta, 44
  gnocchi, 97
ponzu sauce, homemade, 85
port wine sauce, 113, 138
Potato Cannelloni with Confit of Duck and
  Roasted Shiitakes, 36
Potato Oyster Ravioli with Aged Zinfandel
  Sauce, 40
Potato and Forest Mushroom Lasagna with
  Chive Sauce, 42
potato(es)
  chips, baked, 17, 49, 101
  jus, 83
  knishes, 63
  as lasagna, 42, 79
  mashed, 34, 101
  not-fried French fries, 83
  ravioli of, with oysters, 40
  Red Rose, 84, 102
  sautéed, 23, 102
  shoestring, 16
  soup, 63
  truffle chips, 34
  White Rose, 84, 95, 102
  Yukon Gold, 73, 95, 102
poultry. *See* chicken; duck
pudding, chocolate croissant, 132

Q

Quartet of Crème Brûlees, 124
quesadillas, chicken, 48

Index

R

rabbit
  jus, 97
  with polenta gnocchi and zucchini
    mousse, 97-98
  sautéed, with artichokes, 57
radicchio, 19, 55
ragoût
  of mushrooms, 106
  of peas and chanterelles, 103
raspberries, in crumble berry pie, 134
ravioli, potato oyster, 40
Real Slow-Roasted Veal Shank with California
  Baby Vegetables and Hand-Picked
  Chanterelles, 95
rhubarb, and strawberry pie, 125
rice, Arborio, 77
risotto, lobster, 76-77
Rockfish, Roasted Whole, Barded with Bay
  Leaves and Sweet Garlic, 73

S

salad
  corn, sautéed potato, and frisée, 23
  duck, 113 (headnote)
  Dungeness crab, 16
  green, with squab and mushrooms, 55
  lobster, 19
  strawberry, 128
salsa, avocado and cilantro, 48
salsify, 75, 119
Santa Barbara Shrimp with Bright Yellow
  Polenta, Pancetta, Asparagus Tips and Shrimp
  Tarragon Jus, 44
Santa Barbara Shrimp with Mashed Potato and
  Potato Truffle Chips, 34
Sardines "A Day in Nice," 46
sauce
  apple-smoked bacon, 56
  Banyuls, for pheasant, 119
  black pepper, 105
  chive, 42
  confit, 101
  horseradish, 17
  lobster bolognese, 76
  mustard and crème fraîche, 16
  nage butter, 137
  orange, 126
  for partridge, 114
  plum tomato, 38
  ponzu, 85
  port wine, 113
  red wine, 40, 45, 106, 119, 138
  for roasted chicken wings, 37

  for sautéed duck liver, 50
  for scallop rolls, 49
  for sweetbreads, 56
  truffle, 39, 52
  Wild Turkey, 132
  Zinfandel, 40
  see also butter; jus
Scallop Roll with Brown Butter Vinaigrette and
  Long Chives, 49
Sculpin with Zucchini Mousse and Plum
  Tomato Sauce, 38
Sea Bass with Creamy Lentils and Garlic
  Infusion, 80-81
seafood
  clams, vinaigrette of, with salmon, 79
  crab, salad of Dungeness, 16
  lobster
    bolognese, 76
    curried, 74
    jus, 76
    nage, 34, 137
    poached ("Harahan"), 41
    risotto, 76-77
    salad, 19
    stock, 41, 44, 74, 76, 137
  oysters, and potato ravioli, 40
  scallops
    with roasted artichokes, 39
    rolls of, 49
  shrimp
    jus, with tarragon, 44
    Santa Barbara, 34, 44
    to prepare, 139
shallots
  fried, 40
  roasted, 55, 138
  to roast, 138
sorbet
  chocolate, 130
  strawberry, 125
  tangerine, 126
soufflés, warm chocolate, 126
soup
  pea, cold, 65
  potato, 63
spinach, 36, 49, 56, 79, 84, 95, 113
  baby, 74, 99
squab
  confit, 54
  with foie gras, 101
  jus, 54, 136
  roasted, with portobello mushrooms, 54
stock
  chicken, 136
  duck, 36

  lobster, 41, 44, 74, 76, 137
  veal, 138
    reduced (demi-glace), 138
  venison, 105
  see also broth; nage
strawberry
  purée, 128
  and Rhubarb Pie with Strawberry Sorbet, 125
  salad, 128
  sorbet, 125
Stuffed Zucchini Flowers with Truffles à la
  Maximin, 52
Sweetbreads Club Sandwich with Apple-Smoked
  Bacon Sauce, 56

T

tangerine sorbet, 126
Terrine of Artichokes with Roasted Garlic and
  Hollywood Roof-Dried Tomatoes, 21-22
tomato(es)
  with ahi tuna, 15
  cherry, 95, 99
  dried, 44, 46
  mousse, 15, 22
  with sardines, 46
  sauce, 38
  to dry, 21
  to peel, seed, and cut, 139
truffle(s)
  black, in sauce, 39, 52
  jus, 39, 52
  and potato chips, 34
  to prepare, 139
  with zucchini flowers, 52
turnips, baby, 95, 99

V

vanilla
  crème brûlée, 124
  ice cream, 134
veal
  calves' brains, 45
  shank
    poached (osso bucco), 99
    slow-roasted, 95
  stock, 138
  sweetbreads, club sandwich of, 56
vegetable(s)
  baby, with veal shank, 95
  nage, 42, 137
  with osso bucco, 99
  spring, with lobster, 19
  see also individual vegetables

Venison
  Medallions with Persimmons and Celery Root
    Mousse and Black Pepper Sauce, 105
  stock, 105
vinaigrette
  balsamic, 23
  brown butter, 49
  chive, 57
  clam, 79
  walnut, 54
vinegar
  balsamic, 23, 45, 49, 57
  champagne, 54

W

walnut(s)
  in salad, 55
  vinaigrette, 54
Warm Chocolate Soufflés with Tangerine Sorbet
  and Citrus Sauce, 126
Warm Tower of Portobello Mushrooms,
  Foie Gras and Roasted Squab Breast with Its
  Vinaigrette, 54-55
Whitefish, Seared, with French Fries "Not Fried,"
  Roasted Garlic and Brandade, 83
Wienerschnitzel of Artichoke with Roasted Rabbit
  Loin and Chive Vinaigrette, 57
wine sauce, 106, 138
  Banyuls, with pheasant, 119
  port, 113
  Zinfandel, 40
wonton skins, deep-fried, 85

Y

yogurt, drained, 65

Z

zest, candied citrus, 128
zucchini
  flowers, stuffed, 52
  mousse, 38, 52, 97

LIEGGI

COOKBOOK

Joachim Splichal is internationally renowned as one of the most innovative and talented chefs in America. Th[...] been a buzz surrounding Patina, his Los Angeles restaurant, since its opening in 1989, and the enthusiastic m[...] shakers and glitterati continue to flock to his tables. *Patina Cookbook: Spuds, Truffles and Wild Gnocchi* is a celebration of Splichal's culinary genius as well as an exciting, revealing look at his award-winning restaurant.

In *Patina Cookbook*, sixty of Splichal's delicious, whimsically conceived recipes have been meticulously adapted for the home chef. Such temptations as Terrine of Artichokes with Roasted Garlic Cloves and Hollywood Roof-Dried Tomatoes, Santa Barbara Shrimp with Mashed Potatoes and Potato Truffle Chips, and Lemon Sandwich with Candied Citrus Zest and Strawberry Salad are available without waiting for a reservation. As a companion to the recipes and gorgeous, full-color food photographs, there is the engaging story of a typical day for Splichal, illustrated with striking documentary-style photographs. *Patina Cookbook* offers readers a unique, behind-the-scenes tour of the dynamic restaurant that has made Splichal so famous.

"If Oscars were awarded for cooking, Joachim Splichal would have to bunk out in the garage to make room for them in his house." —NEW YORK TIMES

"In Los Angeles, Splichal is a Mozart among the Mendelssohns of the kitchen, a chef whose ideas are closely monitored by other chefs." —GOURMET

"Food this good is a thrill to eat; it reminds you how glad you are to be alive. And it makes you eager for the next taste." —LOS ANGELES TIMES

JOACHIM SPLICHAL is the executive chef-owner of five restaurants in Los Angeles—the award-winning Patina, Pinot Bistro, Patinette at the Museum of Contemporary Art, Cafe Pinot and Pinot Hollywood—as well as one restaurant in the Napa Valley, Pinot Blanc. Splichal was raised in Spaichingen, Germany, and trained in Nice, France. He and his wife, Christine, have lived in Los Angeles for fourteen years. In 1991 Splichal was voted Best Chef in California by the prestigious James Beard Foundation, and in 1994 the Zagat Restaurant Survey crowned Patina the number one restaurant in Southern California for the third year in a row.

Cover design by Renato Stanisic
Food and back cover author photographs by Patrice Meigneux
Black-and-white author photograph by David Stork

Collins Publishers
A Division of HarperCollins Publishers
http://www.harpercollins.com

Printed in the U.S.A.

US $18.00 / $25.50 CAN
ISBN 0-00-649075-1

9 780006 490753   51800

0697